ARTHUR W. PINK

Letters of an Itinerant Preacher

1920-1921

Edited by

RICHARD P. BELCHER

Richbarry Press

P.O. Box 302 Columbia, S.C. 29202

CONTENTS

Explanations

We have sought to preserve the language of Arthur W. Pink in the letters; therefore, some sentences are incomplete, as he wrote in abbreviated form. Some abbreviated words have been completed for understanding, but others (if clear in meaning) have been left as Pink wrote them. Also some punctuations may differ from today's common usage.

We have also sought to make clear persons of whom Pink spoke, if possible. Sometimes he used initials, or failed to use a first name, etc., and several names are not certain as to their full identity.

Brackets [ ] around a word, phrase or paragraph indicate a comment or explanation of the editor.

In the index we have listed the references by the date of the letter (example--2/8/21) rather than by page number.

In most cases we have not sought to correct grammatical or spelling errors, etc., in the letters.

D.V. is an abbreviation for *Deo volente* which means "God willing."

Dr. Richard P. Belcher, Editor

PREFACE

Several years ago the Lord brought me into contact with Dr. W.R. Crews, pastor of the East Gaffney Baptist Church in Gaffney, South Carolina. Dr. Crews was aware of my interest in Arthur W. Pink, and he had driven to Columbia to visit with me. In the course of the conversation he mentioned that he had in his possession a great number of letters that Pink had written to I. C. Herendeen between the years of 1918-1921.

Understandably my interest was perked, and we began discussing the possibility of publishing them. I learned that they had been given to Dr. Crews by Mr. Herendeen, and that he himself had hoped to publish them. Graciously he agreed to send me a copy of them, and then gave me permission to publish them. I do express my sincere thanks and gratitude to Dr. Crews for not only allowing me a copy of these letters, but also for his permission to publish them.

It has taken several years to prepare these letters for publication, as I had to read them, prepare indices for them, and also make a decision whether to publish them in one volume or two. After much thought and prayer, we decided to print them in two volumes, separating the letters into two groups: those written during Pink's ministry in Spartanburg, South Carolina, as a local pastor, and those written by Pink as an itinerant preacher on the west coast. This volume contains the second of the group of letters.

Some may consider the reading of a man's letters (especially the letters of a man already deceased) as a dull and uninteresting experience. Not so if the reader has become acquainted with the writer of the letters in some manner, either personally or through his writings. Most who read these letters of Arthur W. Pink will be those who never had the privilege of knowing him personally, but have experienced the blessing of his writings. Yet even then, the question might come, "Why read the letters of a man who is deceased?"

For one thing, letters can give us a more personal insight into the man and his times. In the case of these letters, they were written in one of the most unusual periods of Pink's life--an hour when he was experiencing immense blessing upon his public ministry of the Word of God. Anyone familiar with Pink knows that during the latter years of his Christian life, he was a failure in public ministry. Doors refused to open! Other doors that opened, quickly closed! And finally he went into isolation. But at the time of the writing of these letters, he was engaged in a very successful itinerant ministry on the west coast. Much of the time he was preaching to hundreds of people in a tent in Oakland, California.

The letters were written to Mr. Herendeen of Swengel, Pennsylvania, Pink's intimate friend and publisher. In them Pink bears his heart concerning many subjects: certain tendencies of the day, certain well-known preachers of the day, etc. Pink had been converted in his hometown of Nottingham, England, about twelve years prior to the writing of these letters.[1] In the years of interval between his conversion and these letters, he had been in the United States, since 1910. He had attended a summer session at Moody Bible Institute in Chicago upon first arriving in America, only to leave in the midst of that semester to journey to Colorado to pastor. From Colorado he trekked eastward to Kentucky where he again pastored, and even got married. By 1917 or 1918 he was found in Spartanburg, South Carolina, as pastor of the Northside Baptist Church.[2]

His letters of this period in South Carolina show that he was quite unhappy the whole time he was there. He longed for another door to open, and even sought to help the Lord

---

[1]For a complete account of Pink's life, see my book titled *Arthur W. Pink: Born to Write,* (Columbia, SC: Richbarry Press, 1991).

[2]See a companion volume of Pink's letters during this era of his life titled *Arthur W. Pink: Letters from Spartanburg, (1918-1920)* (Columbia, SC: Richbarry Press, 1991).

open that door. Finally, when no door would open, he decided to move to Swengel, Pennsylvania, close to his friend, I.C. Herendeen. He even planned to build a house there. But the Lord had other plans, as He opened the door to public ministry in the west; and Pink went with great delight to pursue this new opportunity.

Some of his meetings in the local churches were successful, others were not. He fretted frequently about the demands on his time in this public ministry which left him with little time to study and write. Perhaps his greatest delight were the days he preached in a tent in Oakland, California. A young evangelist from Seattle, Washington, named Brother Thompson, had tremendous success in the city of Oakland under the tent, even drawing hundreds together, with many being converted to Christ. Realizing that they needed nurturing and teaching, he invited Pink to come to the tent to speak. Pink was in the tent preaching and teaching every night of the week on two occasions--August 25, 1920, through October 8, 1920, and then again beginning about February 1, 1921 and running several weeks, perhaps even into the latter part of April. He states in his April 21, 1921, letter (the last letter of this series) that it is now practically certain that they (he and Mrs. Pink with Brother Thompson) will go to Seattle early the next week.

Pink continued this itinerant ministry, so it seems (though the details are uncertain), until March 3rd of 1925 when he left for Australia. Here he was very successful in public ministry once again--for a time. That success was ended by the Baptist group of Australia, and Pink never again knew success in preaching in public. He did try (and try and try and try), but each attempt seemed to turn sour, until finally he moved into seclusion all the way up to the Outer Hebrides in Stornaway, Scotland, on the Isle of Lewis in September of 1940--never to maintain a public ministry again even until his death on July 15, 1952. His final years were devoted to writing!

The reading of all material is somewhat subjective. Perhaps some would feel there can be found in these letters a hint of some of the reasons for the eventual failure of Pink's public ministry--his personality; his longing to spend less time with people and more time writing; or his bull-dogged spirit concerning doctrine, especially some areas that were very unpopular in his day.

Pink in this time of his life was an ardent Calvinist, but he was also a dispensationalist. Later in his life he rejected the dispensational view, moving to a covenantal position, even embracing an amillennial viewpoint, though he did not want to be called by that term. But he never did leave his strong Calvinistic theology--the same theology that is evidenced in these letters.

The editor has found great joy in reading and preparing these letters for printing, along with the preparation of the index material. May they be read with the realization that A.W. Pink was a man like all of us--a man with feet of clay. But it cannot be denied that he was a man God used to revive and renew the doctrines of grace among many of His people in the last half of this twentieth century. In the unfolding of the work, many people are mentioned by name--Pink's friends, those who ordered his books, etc. If any reader has knowledge of any of these persons or the events or places of these letters, or any other letters or information pertaining to Arthur W. Pink, the editor would like to hear from you. Address me at 215 Spartan Dr., Columbia, SC 29212.

Dr. Richard P. Belcher, Editor

PINK'S SCHEDULE
Places and Dates
July 1920-April 1921

1920

Middle of July 1920--Left Pennsylvania for California

Arrived in California on a Monday (no date given)

July 27-August 7	Meeting in Garden Grove, CA
August 8-15	Meeting in Orange, CA
August 16-?(several days)	Meeting in San Francisco under the auspices of National Bible Institute and a Brother Stearnes
August 22 AM	Preached in a Baptist Church, San Francisco
August 22 Afternoon	Preached in a Congregational Church, San Francisco
August 22 PM	Preached in Oakland in Brother Thompson's tent for first time
August 25-September 8	Ministry each evening in Oakland in the tent, forcing him to re-schedule several meetings already booked these days
September 9-12	Meeting in Shafter, CA
September 13-19	Meeting in Anaheim, CA

September 20-25	Rest at Manhatten Beach, CA
September 26-October 1	Meeting at Riverside, CA
October 3-8	Meeting at Pasadena, CA
October 10-15	Meeting at Santa Barbara, CA
October 17-24	Meeting at Long Beach, CA
October 25	Left California for Pennsylvania in afternoon
October 30	Arrived home in Pennsylvania
November 1-21	Home (as far as is known)
November 22-27?	Peddic Memorial Church Newark, NJ
November 28? through early January	At Home

1921

January 13	Arrived back in Oakland, CA
February 1-April 14 or so	Preaching in tent in Oakland

1 The Journey to California and Early Impressions

Garden Grove, California

Arthur W. Pink Swengel, Pa
Author and Bible Teacher

July 28/20

Beloved Brother in the Lord:

Many thanks for yours [your letter] of the 22nd with enclosures all safely to hand yesterday. I return checks endorsed, please to credit of my account with you. Please send two complete sets of my writings to Dr. Stephenson, Albany, Ky. Regarding these, and any other orders which may come to hand during my absence, fill entirely from your own stock--the only thing I would like to adjust later will be the Kingdom of Heaven booklets.

We arrived safely Monday noon. I took a severe cold on the train--head full of it and so hoarse I could only just manage to speak last night--1st of the meetings. The brethren hired the picture-show hall: it is used only Wednesday and Saturday nights so I shall use it, DV, other nights. Advertised to begin Thursday, but a few were so eager I began last night: 35 present (only a few knew of it); spoke on three-fold salvation. Had great liberty. Don't know yet how things may develop: new pastor not yet on field but expect he will preach here Sunday. Met the one who has just moved from here--Brother Francis--not yet "sized him up." Nothing definite yet beyond preaching here till August 7 and then at Orange over 15th. Think, however, the way will be opened up at Santa Ana and Anaheim. My old friend Gwynne Lewis came over yesterday afternoon and remained till this morning: he has already fixed up 8 days meetings for me at Riverside, California, in which most of the churches are uniting--A.C. Gabelein is there end of this week. Lewis believes the Lord may keep me in

Riverside two full weeks at least; the last week to counteract the teaching of my old friend Dr. Mabie there (Universal Reconciliation), which, he tells me, is being widely accepted by the Lord's people in Riverside. I heard this A.M. that Dr. Mabie is coming here to Garden Grove this week for the express purpose of seeing me! He vows he will "convert" me. The Lord grant me light and grace. The bottom is out of everything out here too! Brother Lee is very anxious for me to spend a week at Bible Institute in Los Angeles--he can secure me an opening if I will say the word--am looking to the Lord for guidance. Am sure I am going to get all the work here I can manage this next few weeks: pray daily I may be clearly guided: believe I shall have best sale of books in Riverside. Writing is not going to be easy--so many calling on me and insisting I call on them between meetings: but will try and keep you posted.

Has the Chicago second-hand book store sent the Hebrew Grammar yet?

Will you please forward to me my own copy of God's Sovereignty--it is on the top shelf of the second book case counting from the front door--I feel I must make a start on it; after I leave Garden Grove shall have a little more leisure.

Sorry to hear Brother Smith is so sick, but not surprised.

Have written to S. Riley, a non-committal letter, seeking to draw him out: strange how such letters, one after the other are all coming along right now.

Excuse these disconnected sentences--best I can manage.

With best wishes,
Yours by grace alone,
AWP

P.S. Please send to Mrs. W.C. Goad, Hotel Halbrook, Dickson,Tenn, 2 three-folds; 2 new births, 2 Godhoods, and 1 Mary. (She sent 50 cents too much.)

2 Opposition in Difficult California

Garden Grove, California

Arthur W. Pink
Author and Bible Teacher

Swengel, Pa

July 29/20

Mr. I. C. Herendeen,
Beloved Brother in the Lord:

I enclose endorsed check for $5.00. Please deposit to my credit in running account with you.

Am very thronged, and writing is difficult, and I'm getting quite a few letters.

Am experiencing quite a little open opposition here in Garden Grove but I believe by the end of next week the Lord will overcome Satan's opposition. Am having much liberty in preaching--praise the Lord. Nearly recovered from heavy cold.

My dearest friend here, Harry Lee, who has rigidly followed Mauro's teaching on "Healing" the last ten years, has a daughter of 12 who is afflicted with similar mysterious fits to Norman! He is quite satisfied it is "Demon possession." I expect to be in his home next week, and hope to study closely her case. He has cried and cried to the Lord, but she gets worse and worse--is now paralyzed. He is at his wits end. The Devil works more openly in California than anywhere I've ever been: one can sense and feel his awful presence.

Best wishes, as ever,
Affectionately,
Yours by grace alone,
AWP

3 Pressured by People and a Full Schedule

Arthur W. Pink Swengel, Pa
Author and Bible Teacher

Garden Grove,Calif

Aug 5/20

Beloved Brother in the Lord:

Letter writing is impossible here--hurried notes are the best I can manage. So many want me in their homes to have long talks, and as soon as one is finished with me another is waiting. The high pressure will slacken a little (I trust) when I am through here in Garden Grove.

The Lord is opening many doors--difficulty is to crowd all in. I am already booked up <u>every day</u> (two, yet tentative) till September 12. It looks now as though I shall be out here well into October.

You will rejoice to know that Mr. Jurkin had us in his home last night for supper, and told me to select as many books out of the library of his revered father as I desired. He pressed it on me--I never even mentioned it, this time. I selected 42 books!!! Praise the Lord!

Please send a copy of my "Sovereignty" to Miss May Lowe, Lansdowne Mission, Somkele, Zululand, South Africa, and charge it to my account. Also will you please send me, say twenty sheets of my note paper, same size as this page: you will find them in a big red cardboard box in spare room, on top of second shelf--second of two rough, long ones, I nailed up.

Trust things are going along better with you now. Will try and read carefully what you wrote and return with a few comments in the next few days.

Hurriedly, but cordially
AWP (Please send a few gummers.)

4 California Is Full of Preachers of All Kinds

Mr. I. C. Herendeen Orange, Cal.
Beloved Brother in the Lord Aug 10/20

Your good letter of third and fourth to hand yesterday afternoon. I am still finding it very difficult to secure time for private correspondence--I am having to write quite a few letters here and there, arranging meetings in various places, and planning dates, so as not to conflict. Thanks for attending to my requests regarding orders etc. My cold is considerably better, but not gone. Have not heard further from Dr. Riley yet--DV. will let you know particulars when I do.

Was indeed very, very sorry, and saddened to learn of conditions in [word rubbed out by Herendeen]. My heart goes out to you, dear Brother, and my earnest prayers for you. I am sure you are right in the stand you took, and am also sure God will yet deal severely with [name rubbed out by Herendeen]. I believe it would be well if you were to definitely ask Him to "deal" with [name rubbed out], seeing you are helpless to. It is indeed deplorable, but "blessed are they which are persecuted for righteousness sake" (Matt. 5:10)--note, "are" is in italics: without this word, the state is an abstract one, put thus to include the future as well--"Blessed (shall be) they who are persecuted" etc. I think this must be its primary force. Your lot and trial is by no means unique--everywhere conditions are tragic, I mean among the professing people of God. In Garden Grove things defy description. The Devil sure has got in his work there. One of my old friends there had his wife separate from him six months ago, and I believe they are real Christians. Many are the families there who are divided. I have but two words for you (may our Father bless them to you)--"This poor man cried unto the Lord"--whether or not He may see fit to "deliver" you out of "all your troubles" you must leave to Him; and "Endure hardness as a good soldier of Jesus Christ."

The meetings in Garden Grove were a sorry fizzle: quite a number came, and attended them, from neighboring towns, but only a handful of the Garden Grove people. Average attendance 50.

Last Thursday afternoon, at his request, I spent 2 hours with Dr. Mabie. He "held the floor" nine tenths of the time: he said little that was new to me. About all he said in reply to my objections was: yes, I argued thus for years, but when you have studied the Scriptures as long as I have you'll see differently; you may not see Final Reconciliation now, but you will, etc. There are very, very few of the orthodox pastors out here who any longer believe, still less teach the Eternal punishment of the lost. Dr. Francis, in whose home I'm now staying, believes in Annihilation. Hundreds of God's children round here are all mixed up, and don't know what they believe. The confusion is terrible. Men like Hadden and Farr, seem to preach only on Prophecy--man's ruin, and God's grace; indoctrination of believers is utterly neglected! I'm glad I came out here, and may remain through October.

I came to Orange last Sunday morning, and preached twice that day, and also last night (evening meetings only, thus far), and had great liberty and a fine hearing. Next Sunday night, I am to preach, DV, at a union service of all the evangelical churches of the town, probably to a 1000 people. I expect to spend most of the hour on the Sinner's Ruin! When I came here I expected to conclude next Sunday night, but Brother Francis believes the increasing interest will require me to remain most, if not all, of next week in Orange.

I was in Los Angeles last Tuesday and went round to the Institute. Tried to see Horton, who has the arranging of speakers at "The Church of the Open Door" during Torrey's absence. He was in the building but not approachable. However, he appointed an hour to meet me--12 o'clock; I was at the appointed place at 11:55 and waited till 12:20 but he did not show up, so I left in disgust. I took dinner in the Institute Cafeteria, and then met A. C. Gabelein--he was cordial: I told him I would like to preach in Torrey's church ("Open Door") and he said hold open Sunday August 29--

I'll write you in a few days--so I'm doing as he asked and am awaiting his letter.

August 30 to September 5 I'm booked for Anaheim and may stay through the 7th--am sure shall get a fine hearing there--God has some choice saints in that place: a returned missionary from China broken down in health, has a Bible class there with 75 regular members! September 8 to 12 inclusive I am in Riverside, DV. Am in touch with quite a few other places, but nothing definite fixed yet. But it looks as though I shall be out here well into October: I'm hoping Riley won't want to assume before November.

Was not a bit surprised to hear Victor was marrying so soon, and I think that everything considered, you said the right things to him. On the whole I think it is just as well that Brother Smith is leaving--the Lord deal graciously with him. Has that Brother you thought might be Street's successor, visited you yet? If not, are you expecting him?

Surprised you've heard nothing from A. F. C.'s [Brother Cowles] lawyer--evidently they are consulting with Mauro. By the way, I learned that the Institute teachers are almost solidly believers in Mauro's kingdom teaching.

Shall be glad to hear, as soon as possible what the printers told you.

Pray daily that I may be preserved, guided, empowered, blessed, and used by God to His glory, the eternal blessing of His people, and the salvation of lost sinners. Rest assured I shall pray daily for you.

With love in Him,
Yours by grace alone
AWP

5 Disappointing Meetings, But Still Hopeful

Orange, Cal.
Aug 13/20

Beloved Bro in the Lord:

Yours of the 5th duly to hand, enclosing the letter from Brother Kilgore--herewith returned. You did quite right in crediting my account with $5.00 from him.

Am still fearfully rushed. Through here at 6 Sunday night, the 15th. On the 16th, DV, I shall go to Frisco to Stearnes (at his request) for a week's meetings under the auspices of N. B. I. [National Bible Institute] , and I may remain there 10 or 12 days. At Anaheim Aug 30 to Sept 5 inclusive.

Meetings at Orange rather disappointing: little interest: average attendance 50 to 60; but hope to preach to 500 or 600 Sunday night--union service. Dr. Francis here, late of Garden Grove, believes in Annihilation and never preaches on Eternal Punishment! So it goes. The Lord keep you and me faithful. It is real hot here: felt no "quakes" yet. It will be much cooler in Frisco, for which I'm glad. My copy of Sovereignty to hand--thanks. Hope to crowd in some work on it.

Hastily, but affectionately,
AWP

6 Dead Churches and Meetings, But a Challenging Invitation to Oakland

San Francisco, California

Mr. I. C. H. Aug 23/20
Beloved Bro:

If you knew the heavy strain I am under continually, you would make full allowance for my seeming carelessness in writing you infrequently.

Since last writing, there have been quite unexpected and most blessed developments. The meetings here in the Institute have been rather disappointing: interest small: though a few have been blessed I am sure. Last Thursday afternoon there was present at my meetings a Brother Thompson, late of Seattle, now travelling evangelist with a huge tent. He spoke to me at the close of the meeting and said: "Brother Pink, I've been to Oakland with my tent for 3 months: there have been over 150 genuine converts, and in addition some 400 to 500 more of the Lord's people have gathered around me. I've now brought them along as far as I am able, but I'm no teacher, and they sorely need a teacher, for hundreds of them are but babes in Christ. I believe you are God's man for them. I gladly place my tent freely at your disposal, and will do all in my power to support you. Won't you come." It fairly took my breath away! I said I was very sorry but I was all booked up for this next month. He said October would be too late--rains begin end of September. I offered Brother Thompson Sunday night which was all I had open during the time I was to be in Frisco.

Yesterday (Sunday), I preached in one of the Baptist churches of Frisco: about 150 present, but dead as a door nail! In the afternoon spoke for an hour at the Congregational Church (where S. D. Jordan's brother is pastor) under auspices of N. B. I.--about 75 out: had a glorious and most blessed time--spoke on grace as per 2nd address at Harrisburg. In the evening went over to Oakland to Thompson's tent. I got there 10 minutes before time to begin, and the place was packed out. Every one of the 1000 seats was occupied and scores standing. By the time to begin, one of the sides had to be raised. I spoke for 65 minutes along the lines of my tract "The Way of Salvation." The people listened with breathless interest throughout--over 1200! O how I praise God for such a blessed opportunity and privilege.

Brother Thompson begged me to reconsider my decision. Said he would guarantee me 500 (at least) deeply interested, hungry babes in Christ, eager for the Word, every night, and over a 1000 Saturday and Sunday nights. I asked him to give me 12 hours to pray over it.

By this A.M. it seemed that this was a call from God, so I have written to the places where I am to hold my next 4 meetings, DV (Shafter, Anaheim, E. Hollywood, and Riverside) asking them to put forward my dates 1 week with the possibility of 2 weeks for me to let them know later. So Wednesday night, DV, I begin at Thompson's tent. I expect to confine myself to Doctrinal Exposition! It will be a tremendous strain, for I already feel very noticeably the effects of speaking 2 to 3 times every day without a break for this last month, and 3 weeks before I came to Frisco, it was terribly hot; and speaking in a huge tent is very trying; but I am trusting the Lord to "sustain" me. Pray earnestly and definitely, please, beloved, and join me in devout praise to our God of all grace for Himself proffering His most unworthy servant a golden opportunity --Ps 34.

Excuse pencil: I am writing in bed with my back against the pillows trying to snatch a little rest after a heavy day's work--it is not 11 P. M. I hope to be a help, under God, to Thompson. He is a dear Bro., and I sincerely hope teachable. Expect Brothers Ironside and Crain will be back in Oakland by end of this week. How strange that Brother Thompson should insist that I am God's man for his tent when these brethren will be to hand. Surely this is the Lord's doing, and it is wonderful in my eyes.

God bless you, dear Bro, and supply your every need, according to His riches in glory by Christ Jesus. Amen.

Affectionately, AWP

7 Thousands Hear the Word in Oakland

Oakland, California

1817 Telegraph Ave., Oakland

Aug 27/20

Beloved Brother in the Lord:

Am having a glorious time here. The most wonderful opening and opportunity I have ever had: 700 people nightly; over a 1000 Saturday and Sunday--all deeply interested, hungry for the Word. Bro Thompson is anxious I should remain on for some time (indefinitely) and teach. Expecting C.C. Crain and Brother Ironside here next week, and then!!--Sov!!! The Lord use me to His glory.

Affectionately
Yrs by Grace
AWP

8 Crowds Increasing in Oakland

Western Book and Tract Co.
1817 Telegraph Ave., Oakland, Calif.

Aug 30/20

Beloved Brother:

The meetings here are affording much cause for fervent praise: have never seen anything quite like them before: the interest is genuine, deep, and wide spread. Am sure there are scores of sinners really seeking the Lord and hundreds of the saints being built up. Numbers steadily increasing: last night between 1200 and 1500 listened for 80 minutes while the Lord helped me wonderfully to speak on Christ's Return. Bro Thompson and others have urged me to remain a second week at least, and it is far too good and grand an opportunity to miss; I cannot, but accept. I shall be here, therefore, till the 8th of September, DV.

I wish you could have witnessed a scene yesterday AM. I went to the "Grant" meetings here--about 100 present--but sat right at the back and refused to break bread with them. Brother T [Thompson] and Mr. Crane came and had a long talk with me: they were simply "flabbergasted" when I told them I was a member of a Baptist Church because I considered they were more Scriptural than those known as "the Brethren." I "took the bull by the horns" and told them they were unscriptural on a number of points: that apart from I Cor 14 which deals with the regulation of "tongues" and "prophesying" there was nothing whatever for "an open meeting." I held my ground quite easily, they had no Scripture with which to refute me. I pressed on them Acts 9:26 and they both admitted they had never weighed the "joined." At the end of this week there is the annual Brethren Conference. C. C. Crain from Boston and H.A. Ironside will be here--I expect to have it "up and down" with them on Sovereignty and Reprobation. Bro T is pretty sound on Sov, and I've satisfied him that God "loves" only His elect people, and he is more than half convinced on Reprobation.

Am praying much for you: don't give a second thought to leaving the Bible Truth Depot--that is not of God I'm sure: the Lord sustain your faith. Have not time to enter into detail, but the enclosed does not appeal to me at all.

Affectionately,
AWP

9 Books Are Selling!

Arthur W. Pink
Author and Bible
Teacher

SWENGEL, PA
Mon Septr 6/20

Beloved Brother:

Please forward as soon as possible one complete set (including Gos. [Gospel] pamphlets of mine) to each as below:

Mrs. R.E. Dooling, General Del. Richmond, California
Mr. Geo Duckworth, 1254 64th St., Oakland, "
Miss Lockhart, 1526 7th Ave, " "
Mr. Geo McConnell, 1526 7th Ave, " "

I have enclosed two cheques, one for $5.00 and the other for $15.00. Please credit my account.

Hurriedly but affect,
AWP

10 The Most Strenuous But Glorious Time of His Life

Oakland, Septr 7th/20
Mr. I.C. Herendeen, Beloved Brother:

Am still 'rushed to death': having the most strenuous but glorious time of my life. Bro C. Crain a firm believer in Eternal Reprobation and absolute Sovereignty of God but takes issue with me on Limited Atonement. Had little opportunity yet to have a talk with Ironside. Thompson goes with me all the way! Orders are coming in fine for the books--praise the Lord! Please supervise filling of orders below--one complete set to each.

Mr. L. H. Foskett, 5107 Shafter Ave, Oakland, Cal.
Mr. W.A. Griffith, 560 20th Street, " "
Mrs J. Carlson, 35 Rose Ave, " "
Mrs. M. Anderson, 2222 Piedmont Ave, Berkeley, Cal
Mr. J.B. Arthur, 1920 Primrose Ave, So. Pasedena, "
Mr. L.H. Swenson, 1829 Market St, Oakland, "
Miss E. Youngquist, 613 Jones St, " "
Mr. J.G. Jensen, 875 Pine St " "
Mr. J. Lavender, 2919 Schadack Ave, Berkeley, "
Mr. Aubrey Fair, 530 41st St, Oakland, "
Miss C. High, 1435 Funston Ave, San Francisco, "
Mr. A.P. Sprague, 5507 College Ave, Oakland, "
Mrs. H.W. Chapman, 2431 Dwight Way, Berkley, "
W. Johannsen, 4834 Telegraph Ave, Oakland, "
Theo Koot, 1173 Regent St, Alameda, "
Nick Gooson, 1173 " " " "
Mr. G.G. Baehr, 1342 62nd Ave, East Oakland, "
Mrs. J.C. Johnson, 116 Glen Ave, Coalinga, "
Mrs. A.R. Ackerman,138 Hayden St, Healdsburg, "
Mrs. C.W. Carpenter, 116 Montgomery St, Oroville "
F. Dryer, 1935 Stuart St, Berkeley, "
M. Vollhrecht, 2648 34th Ave, Oakland, "
P.W. Olson, 228 Wayne Avenue, " "
Miss L.A. Allen, Mount View " "
Mrs. Y. Alvers, 1922 Broadway. Alameda, "
Mr. Nels Thompson, 1817 Telegraph Ave, Oakland, "

Well, I guess this list will make you gasp--twenty-seven sets in all--and probably more to follow. I enclose two cheques, one for $75.00 and other for $25.00 which please place to my credit.

Hurriedly but affect,
AWP

11 No Time to Tell of the Blessings in Oakland

Oakland
Septr 8/20

Beloved Brother:

I had wondered what you said and thought when you received mine of yesterday along with the long list of orders, and what you will say when you go through this. I wish I could snatch 1/2 an hour to describe to you in some detail the "wonderful works of God" here in Oakland this last two weeks, but it is utterly impossible. Please forward one complete set of my writings (including one each of the Gospel tracts) to the following, charging same to my account:

Mrs. K.L. Bliss, 3154 Elm St., Oakland, Cal
Adolph Schwyler, Agricultural Hall, University of Cal, Berkeley
H. Guthrie 1515 Webster St., Oakland, Cal
Mr. A. Holzaphel, 1740 Franklin St, " "
Mr. S.J. Nelson, 15519 McMillan Ave, " "
J.M. Taulbee, 184 9th St. " "
Mr. J. Field, 586 63rd St " "
P.L. Lebo, 453 66th St. " "
Miss G.F. Vore, 2226 Haste St., Berkeley, Cal
Mrs E. Kennedy, 526 18th St., Oakland, Cal
Mr. R. Painter, 2820 Summit St., " "
Miss L. Estrem, 1120 Taylor St., San Francisco, Cal
F.D. Harrison, 1059 Santa Clara Ave, Alameda, "
Mrs. I. Easson, 547 E. 12th St, Oakland, "
Mrs. C. D. Kaufman, 136 11th St " "
Mrs. J.N. Crosby, 4805 Virginia Ave. " "
Mrs. R. Albert, 2434 E. 21st St. " "
Mr. S. Swoboda, 1530 23rd Ave, " "
Mrs. C.W. Place, 2240 Telegraph Ave, Berkeley, "
Mrs. A. Mason, 233 Webster St, Oakland, Cal
Mrs. C. Bender, 2635 23rd Ave, " "

Mr. W. Cane, 583 Sycamore St, " "
Mrs. G. MacKenzie, 622 Oak St, " "
S.E. Ward, 1811 Delaware, Berkeley, "
Miss J. Steven, 1515 Webster St, Oakland, "
Mr. C. F. Daugherty, 1728 West St. " "
P. Magnuson, 50 Fairmont Ave, " "
Mrs. D. S. Kelly, 1315 Myrtle " "
Mrs. A. M. Larsen, 822 33rd St. " "
Mr. W.A. Griffith, 560 20th St., " "
Mrs. Barker, 2212 Rosedale Ave, " "
Mrs. H. Johnson, 3903 Quigley, " "
Mrs. L. Jewell, 2322 1/2 Steisant St, Berkeley, Cal
Miss A. Rutherford, 696 Mariposa Ave, Oakland, "
W.R. Fairfield, c/o 1817 Telegraph Ave, " "
Mrs., Banta, 2206 9th Ave, " "
Mrs. T.G. Van Booskirk, 250 Wilwood Ave, Piedmont, Cal
Mr. Werner, Box 64, Oakland, Cal - two sets
C.E. Carlson, 1941 Berkeley Way, Berkeley, Cal - two sets
P.S. Barker, Manteca, Cal

In addition to the above "shipping order" (!) please send ten each of my books and twenty-five each of my booklets and tracts to the Western Book and Tract Co., 1817 Telegraph Ave., Oakland, Cal, and send [word not clear]. Please see to it that these orders are filled satisfactorily. I leave here in the morning for Shafter: booked up solid to Oct 14 and half a dozen other places waiting me. Am enclosing draft for $ 200 which please place to my credit: if balance in hand hold it to cover next orders I hope to send.

Affect.
AWP

The securing of these orders represents considerable work and time.

PPS Of course I shall <u>not</u> want any royalty from the Western Book and Tract Co.'s order--they are doing a <u>heavy</u> business and I believe this order will lead to many others, DV.

12 Sorrowful to Have Had to Close in Oakland

Shafter, Cal
Sep 10/20

Mr. I.C. Herendeen,
Beloved Brother in the Lord:

I closed at Oakland on Wed night (the 8th), tho' the friends there begged and urged me to remain longer. I had gladly done so, but for the fact I was assured the Lord had a work for me in other places. I received another large batch of orders for my writings the last night I was in Oakland, as below:--please send one set of my writings to each of the following including tracts:--

Mrs. Philip Green, R. 2, Box 208, Chico, Cal.
Mrs. W.C. Louis, 4016 Piedmont Ave., Oakland, Cal.
Mrs. S. Jackson, 594 - 19th St, " "
Mrs. Ida Vailes, 9622 e. 14th St. " "
Mr. W. T. Montgomery, 110 Stillman St., San Fran., "
Dr. R. M. Close-Eckert, 1777 Franklin St., Oakland, Cal
Mrs. V. Williams, 28 Harvard Apts, 542 25th St , " "
Mrs. M.A. Owen, 1605 E. 21st St. " "
Mr. C.D. Hart, 651 Jean St " "
Miss E. Pyentz, 453 66th St. " "
Mr. E.G. Griffiths, 624th St. " "
Mrs. A.K. Miller, 1338 Hattuck Ave, Berkeley, Cal
Mrs. C. Mattson, 1607 Grant St. " "
Miss S. Hardesty, 2439 Dwight Wa " "
Mrs. Hugh Shaw, 604 William St. Oakland, "
Mrs. C. Hettyoh, 1822 Brush St. " "
Mr. J.S. Desmond, 3801 Brighton Ave., " "
Mrs. G. Harvey, 1511 Aldine St. " "
Mrs. A. Wibeck, 19 - 8th St. " "
Mrs. W. J. Proctor, 566 William St. " "
Mrs. H. McKeone 1526 - 7th Ave " "
Miss S. Boyle, 1311 Oak St. Aalmeda, Cal.
Mrs. M. Brignsend, El Cerrito, Contra Costa County, Cal.

C.C. Schemel, 2063 Franklin St, Oakland, Cal
Miss M. DeLesemier, 2520 Warring St, Berkeley, Cal
Mr. J. C. Murphy, 446 Hamilton Ave, Palo Alto, "
G. K. Chapman, San Francisco Theological Seminary, San Anselmo, Cal
Soren Jensen 1202 Colusa Ave, Berkeley, Cal
Mr. R. Boyd 580 43rd St., Oakland, "
Mr. Dave Albert, Santa Rosa Ave. " "

I am indeed profoundly thankful to the Lord for creating such a demand, and that He who, by grace, enabled me to write and you to publish, should now lay it on the hearts of so many to order. I believe this sale of over 100 sets in Oakland is a sure indication that God is not through with either of us. "Be of good cheer", dear brother--<u>you</u> are engaged in a most needful and blessed work, 'blessed' because <u>His</u>! Let not Satan turn you aside, for try to he certainly will.

I had a most pleasant surprise here last night: Shafter is only about three times the size of Swengel, and I was not expecting more than 30 or 40 out, but there were well over 150, and they listened closely. I am expecting to enclose bank draft for $120 in this--please place to my credit to cover these orders: kindly supervise (as far as possible) the filling of these orders, especially the addressing of them. Also please let me know how my account stands with you, after this list of orders has been filled and after enclosed is placed to my credit.

With cordial greetings,

Yours by Grace,

AWP

13 Blessings in Shafter and Future Plans

Arthur W. Pink
Author and Bible
Teacher

Anaheim
Sept. 15th, 1920

Mr. I. C. Herendeen,
Beloved Bro in the Lord:

I arrived here safely Monday night at 7 o'clock (just 30 minutes before service time) after travelling 175 miles in an auto over all kinds of roads for 12 hours. Had splendid meetings at Shafter: was most agreeably surprised: Shafter is so small a place, I expected only small crowds; but had 200 or 250 Thursday, Friday and Saturday nights and over 400 on Sunday! Here we started with 40 Monday night, and 70 last night. Am going over today to Pasadena to see Dr. Pratt (once a fellow-worker with Tucker--a strong Bullingerite) to arrange a meeting in his church.

Yes it was strange how Bro Thompson should prefer me to do the teaching in his tent when Ironside and other "Brethren" teachers were there to hand. But God over-ruled I am sure. Bro Thompson said he felt irresistibly drawn toward me. He is an exceptionally fine fellow, though like us, has his defects, of course. Says he will send me two or three hundred dollars worth of tracts from you right away--hope he does, but rather doubt it. I met your friend, Guy Whitney, in Oakland. He was attending the conference. He appeals to me. He gave me a pressing invitation to come to Seattle for the whole month of January for meetings at the Gospel Auditorium. Also met another Brother from Vancouver, named Hunt, who wants me there for two weeks, and a third Bro from Victoria. As near as I can now judge, I believe the Lord may keep us here in California till early in November; then come home for two weeks rest-up; then go to Newark, N.J., if they accept the date I offered them (in response to their inquiry), viz, last week in November, and probably a return visit to Troy's church in Brooklyn; then home for the last one-half of December; and in January, most likely leave for Seattle and neighboring area for 3 months meetings! I want you, please to try your best to arrange and plan ahead to have, say, 200 complete sets of my writings on hand by Feb 1/21--after all the Christmas orders have been filled. I do not believe the Lord is through with you at Swengel, I fully believe the most important of the Lord's work through you at the Bible Truth Depot lies in the near future. I believe Satan knows this, and is trying hard to hinder things: shall continue praying for you.

The enclosed bill has come to hand: there seems to be some little mistake in it--should not the last item in it be just twice as much (instead of 4 times as much) as the first item? Will you kindly pay this for me--after ascertaining the correct amount--and later I will remit, DV.

Both of us are keeping fit, and trusting you are quite well and with best wishes

I remain
Yours by Grace,
AWP

14 Unsure of the Future But Burdened to Write

Manhatten Beach, Calif
September 22nd, 1920

Mr. I.C. Herendeen
Beloved Brother in the Lord:

An old friend in Los Angeles drove Mrs. Pink and I over here last Monday afternoon. Another old friend of mine has a cottage here and kindly offered us the use of it: she and her daughter left the next morning so that my wife and I have the place to ourselves till Saturday morning, when, DV, my friend Gwynne Lewis will come for us in his car and take us to Riverside where my next meeting is scheduled to begin Sunday September 26th, that is, the day following. The "holiday season" is over so that everything here is delightfully quiet: weather is pleasantly cool: cottage is only two blocks from the sea front, and as I write I can hear the noise from the breakers. I do wish you were with us. It is so gracious of the Lord to make this provision for His unworthy servant, for I can tell you I have been "going some" the last 2 months. But it has been happy and blessed work, and I feel none the worse for it.

Your two short letters of the 15th and 16th reached me today. Was glad to learn you had arrived back safely. I, too, feel you ought to be unfeignedly thankful that God has placed you in Swengel, away from so much that is nerve-racking and distasteful. You are having part in a blessed work, dear brother, as I am sure the day will show. Though I have been far too busy to write much to you, nevertheless you have been much on my heart, and I have prayed frequently. Probably my English temperament does much to conceal it, but I assure you I love you much in the Lord. You know there is an old saying that "still waters run deep."

Yes, I thought the lists of orders forwarded from Oakland Wednesday would "astonish" you. I hoped the Lord timed them so as to cheer and establish your heart. I am anticipating many more orders, but one cannot tell. I appointed a Brother as my agent in Anaheim, and I believe he will sell quite a few more books in the future. I much appreciate the fact that you personally made out the labels and supervised the filling out of the orders. Thank you.

Today I received a letter from Bro Thompson inviting me to return to Oakland in two weeks time, but I am unable to respond, nor do I feel it is the Lord's will for me. I do believe, however, that from now on I shall receive numbers of calls for teaching work from various quarters. Have you ever heard of G.P. Raud of 156 5th Ave. N.Y. City, Director of the Russian Bible and Evangelization Society? Through some confusion and mistake in dates, he arrived in Oakland the last Sunday I was there, expecting to speak in the tent that afternoon, as also on the following day--Monday Labor Day. I gladly gave him half of my time and he much appreciated this. He is a dear Brother, deeply taught in the Word. He said from the platform that my book on God's Sovereignty had meant more to him than he could express: he told me in private, he thought he had been able to allay much of A.C.G.s [A.C. Gabelein] prejudice against the book--had recently had a long conversation with him about it while Gabelein was in Los Angeles. Bro Raud has been a Bible teacher in this country for over 10 years before he took up his present work on behalf of Russia, and said he had 3 times as many calls for Bible teaching work than he could possibly fill! Said he was frequently asked to recommend another teacher as a substitute, and after hearing me twice in Oakland said he would be more than pleased to put engagements my way, and begged me to let him know ahead anytime I was to come anywhere around N.Y. as he could easily open several doors for me in those parts. Bro Thompson also writes asking me to keep in close touch with him, as after he leaves Oakland and goes to other places he is anxious for me to come and follow him up after he has done the evangelizing and gotten the crowds together. But I am clear that the Lord would have me devote at least a third of my time to study and writing: only today I read a letter from one who has recently read my book on God's Sovereignty saying how much they had been helped by it, and praising God for it, and I have been told by so many out here of help received from "Gleanings in Genesis" that I feel I must keep them up. I shall have to return to Swengel, DV, before I can finish the revising of God's Sov. I must refer to quite a few of the Puritans' works for quotations and suggestions. I am just criticizing the work here, and trying to see where and how it may be improved.

I think I told you previously, that I offered the Baptist Church at Newark, N.J., the last week in November for a meeting: have not yet heard from them. If they accept, I expect to return to Swengel the 2nd week in November. If they decline, and the demand continues here, may remain in California till the end of the year, though I hardly think that is likely. As the weather is turning cooler, we are in need of some warmer wraps: when we left home we expected to return by the end of September, so I brought no overcoat with me. Will you, therefore, please forward to me, by return post, if possible by Parcel Post, Insured, to Mr. A.W. Pink, % Dr. J. R. Pratt, 517 W. Montana St., Pasadena, Cal:--

1st my light weight, dark colored overcoat, hanging in the spareroom

2nd Mrs. Pink's sweater--the one with belt in, lighter colored of the two

3rd Mrs. Pink's black, high-topped shoes, in shoe-bag, on back of store room door

Kindly, be sure and charge postage to my account. I shall be in Pasadena, DV, from October 3rd to 8th inclusive, so address letters there that week.

Trusting you are now feeling more settled in your spirit, and that conditions are better at home, and that the Lord is blessing His peerless Word to you,

I am,
Affectionately,
Yrs by Grace
AWP

P.S. Please tell Brother Clarence I wish to be kindly remembered to him.

15 Blessed Meetings

Pasadena, California

Monday AM.
October 4th 1920

Mr. I.C. Herendeen
Beloved Brother in the Lord:

The Lord continues to be very gracious unto us: doors are still being opened by Him and His blessing is most marked and manifest. We had a most blessed time in Riverside last week: reached high-water mark on the Wednesday night when I preached for 90 minutes on Justification: there were five preachers present among the congregation and they, too, got thoroughly warmed up, and I trust had their eyes opened to see that there are still numbers left who delight to hear the Word of God preached. This week I am with Dr. Pratt: he is regarded as the strongest expositor of the Scriptures there is on the Pacific Coast: he has quite a large church, made up mostly of the better class, and his congregation is drawn from a radius of 30 to 40 miles--numbers who like his teaching coming in from quite a distance. He is 65 years old: strong Bullingerite, but a very gracious and lovable man. I feel it quite an honor to be teaching in his church: had a good time yesterday morning on "Grace," and last night on "The Cross." Next week, DV, I shall be in Santa Barbara in the Baptist Church where Dr. Catherwood is pastor: he is also spoken of as a strong expositor and pre-millennial. Brother Stearnes recommended me to him. Yesterday, I received an invitation from the largest church in Long Beach, to hold a week's meeting there: I am waiting to hear from San Bernardino as I am wanted there, if dates can be arranged. I expect Long Beach will be the last meeting on this trip, as I am anxious to be back in Swengel by about the 1st week in Nov. Did I tell you that the Peddic Memorial Church, New J (2500 membership) has arranged for me to come and hold a meeting with them the last week in Nov?

Now briefly to reply to your last two letters to hand--18th and 20th. Am glad to learn that all the Oakland orders had been filled when you wrote: it must have crowded you some. I do not anticipate any repetition of the Oakland rush of orders, tho' one never knows: probably there will be quite a good demand here when I mention my writings. I sold several sets in Riverside, but as I knew you were running low on God's Sov. I left this one out (and expect to continue doing so the balance of this trip), and offered the set minus God's Sov. at $4.00 (rather please charge up these sets to my account at $4.00 (less 25%)): please fill the following at your earliest as I should have sent in the orders last Friday--one complete set of my writings (excepting Sov.) to each of the following:

Mr. G. A. Williams, 180 Alta Vista Drive, Riverside, Cal.
Mr. Robt. McMillen, 355 W. 9th Street, " "
Mrs. G. W. Hinste, 223 N. Orange St. " "
Mr. E. J. Polloch, 701 Main St. " "
Dr. H. M. Jamieson, 561 W. 11th St. " "
(include "God's Sov" with this one)
Mr. W.T. Bigger, 183 Linwood Place, Riverside, Cal.
("Redeemer's Return" only)
Miss A. Squire, 496 W. 5th St., Riverside, Cal.
Mr. G.L. Lewis, Box 338, Riverside, Cal. (7 Sayings only)
Mrs. Heron, 234 W. Slawson, Los Angeles, Cal. (")

Thank you for paying my tax bill for me: one other commission for you: will you please ask Clarence to order for me right away one more Book-case, uniform in style and make with the others I had from him--a full-decker, just the same as the other, except in this case I would like the top shelf to be 2 inches deeper than the other four.

No, Bro Thompson has no means whatever of his own, but the Lord supplies him very bountifully. Yes, I believe Guy Whitney is in the same meeting as Bro Thompson: Whitney impressed me very favorably, as a well-balanced, well read, intelligent and lovable believer. Am wondering whether you have heard from the lawyers yet--surely you have by this time.

We expect to return home via Spartanburg, DV, and spend a day or two with Dr. Brown. Trusting you are all keeping well, and with best wishes.

I remain, Affectionately, Yrs by Grace,
Arthur W. Pink

P.S. Will you please order for me the following and charge to my account: G. Thomas on Romans--3 Vols; L. Tucker on Romans--cloth binding; Pettingill on Romans; C. Crain on Romans; Modern Mission Century, and In Christ by A.T. Pierson, and commentary on Hebrews by G.A. Chadwick--one vol. uniform with G. Thomas on Romans.

16 Many Open Doors Now and Tomorrow

Pasadena, California

October 8th, 1920

Beloved Brother:

Your last three letters of September 25 & 28 and October 1st, each safely to hand. Thanks for paying my taxes. No, I did not get an opportunity to speak at the Torrey Inst. Glad to hear the book "The Believer's Life," by Pierson is to hand. Will you please order for me a copy of C. Crain's small book on Romans, from Loizeaux Bros.

Pleased to learn you are now more settled in spirit and better satisfied with the sphere in which God has placed you. I do not believe God has qualified you to teach or preach, but I am sure he has fully equipped you for the work you are now engaged in.

During this week, I have had a very pressing invitation to come back to Oakland right away for a return visit: he says many are praying about it, and numbers feel it is God's will for me to do so. Also, a warm invitation from a Dr.

Southerland of Grace Baptist Church in San Jose, asking me to come to his church for 2 weeks following my return visit to Oakland; but after looking to the Lord, I am quite satisfied He would have me return to Swengel by the end of this month, so have declined both these invitations with thanks. Unless the Lord clearly orders otherwise, I, too, desire to spend at least a third of my time at home studying and writing, tho' I believe this will become more and more difficult as time goes on. Dr. Pratt (at whose church I am now ministering) is intimately acquainted with the head of the Bible School at Binghampton, having lectured there for a month two different years: he asked me yesterday how I would like to have a month there, going systematically thru Romans with 120 students: I said nothing would or could please me more. He said he was sure he could easily get me in there and would write the Principal right away. I believe from now on there will be many open doors and needy fields. Moreover, as I get out in this way, it will mean doubling or that tripling, at least, the sale of my books. Yet, I do hope and expect to continue studying and writing. I've not been idle by any means the last two months: have read seven books last 2 weeks.

I attended to the matter of the two Express packages at Oakland yesterday. Please fill the following orders:--a set to each below, leaving out "God's Sovereignty"--

Mrs. Chas. C. Sterrett, 5428 Walnut Hill Ave., Los Angeles, Cal.
Mrs. E. L. Eldredge, 1457 N. Holliston Ave., Pasadena, Cal.
Mr. G.J. Stuzmann, R.D. 2, Box 423, Pasadena, Cal.
Mr. J.M. Roberts, R.D. 2, Box 288, Pasadena, Cal.
Mr. M. Van Helden, 611 Cypress Ave., Pasadena, Cal.
Mrs. H. R. Dane, R.D. 2, Box 123, Pasadena, Cal.
Dr. J. R. Pratt, 517 W. Montana St., Pasadena, Cal. (include copy "God's Sov.")
Miss B. Pike, 1276 N. Michigan Ave, Pasadena Cal--one each of all my booklets and pamphlets, but no books with this order.

Hope to have a few more orders tomorrow.

Had a glorious time last night on "Sanctification".

You will have to take a day off, when I get back home, DV, to hear all the news: I could write a bulky book on my experiences in California this last 3 months. By the way, speaking of home reminds me, that one flue needs fixing for the coming winter--i.e. some arrangement needs putting in a foot or so above the stove which helps to regulate the draft. Would you kindly see Mr. Snyder, or some competent man, and have this put in right away. Also, if you think our house is damp, would much appreciate it, if you would open windows and doors someday when sun is shining and let it air out well; or put a fire in the stove if you think the house needs it.

Many thanks for the overcoat and etc. all safe to hand and quite O.K.

I enclose check $38.50 which please place to my account.

We are both keeping well, and trust you and yours are ditto.

With best wishes, Affectionately,
Yours by Grace alone,

AWP

P.S. Address me Garden Grove till October 24th.

17 Books Continue to Sell

Pasadena, California
October 9, 1920

Mr. I.C. Herendeen
Beloved Brother in the Lord

Please give careful attention to the following orders: one complete set of my writings (including one each of the Gospel pamphlets of mine), but leaving out "God's Sovereignty", to those below:--

Mr. H. P. Boshoren, 928 Sunset Ave., Pasadena, Calif.
Mrs. M.A. Baldwin, 460 Atlanta St., R.R. 2, Box 217, Pasadena, Calif.
Mrs. E. C. Kuhler, 2145 Lincoln Ave., Box 205, R.R. 2, Pasadena, Calif.
Miss Mary Robertson, 895 N. Los Robles, Pasadena, Calif.
Miss Greenshields, 408 Summit Ave., Pasadena, Calif.
Mr. Orr, 184 E. Colorado, Pasadena, Calif.
Mr. J.M. Roberts, R.F.D. 2, Box 288, Pasadena, Calif.
Miss E.M. Broadbent, 1266 N. Menton Ave., Pasadena, Calif.
Mrs. A.S. Hayton, 515 W. Montana St., Pasadena, Calif.
Mrs. Hoffner, 501 Toolen Place, Pasadena, Calif
" Mary Wisusele, 1946 N. Fair Oaks Ave., Pasadena, Calif.-- R.R. only
M.E. Cook , 1175 Chicoke St., Pasadena, Calif.
Mrs. Eldridgfer, 1457 N. Holliston Ave., Pasadena, Calif.-- as below:

12 copies of New Birth
12 " " Threefold Salv.
12 " each of my Gospel pamphlets.

Closed a very blessed meeting here last night. Praise God for these orders & for all His mercies. I enclose five checks totalling in value $23.00 which please place to my credit.

Affectionately in Him,
AWP

P.S. Charge the sets to me at $4.00 each less discount, the last three orders add 10 cents each for postage.

P.P.S. A sister called round just now with check for a set of my writings--I enclose same making $27.00 in all: please send set to her:--Mrs. M. H. Bartley, 696 W. Dakota St., Pasadena, Cal.

18 Plans to Come Home to Swengel

Garden Grove, Calif.
October 16, 1920

Mr. I.C. Herendeen
Beloved Brother in the Lord:

The Meeting at Santa Barbara was a good one, tho' scarcely up to the level of the previous one at Dr. Pratt's church. Tomorrow, DV, I begin an 8 days meeting at Long Beach: this will be my last for this trip. We plan to leave Garden Grove Monday afternoon October 25th for home, via Chicago--same route we went by, except we intend to come via Harrisburg rather than Pittsburgh. We had thought of coming back by the Southern Route, and dropping off for 36 hours at Spartanburg but find it is further round that way, and would cost $40.00 extra; so have abandoned the idea. By the time you get this letter, we shall almost be ready to start for home.

The Lord has been most gracious in supplying all our need, & we praise Him for His faithfulness. I enclose ten dollars of His "silver & gold", in His name, for your own personal needs--please receive it as from Him. I feel led to send a like amount to Bro. Street by this mail.

We expect to arrive at Swengel, DV, Sat. afternoon October 30th, via Harrisburg. Till then, with best wishes,

Hastily but Cordially,
AWP

19 Still Planning to Come Home to Swengel

Long Beach, Calif.
October 21, 1920

Mr. I.C. Herendeen,
Beloved Brother in the Lord:

We have purchased our tickets & will leave Los Angeles, DV, next Monday night on the Santa Fe & expect to arrive in Swengel Saturday at 2:30. Will you kindly do three things for us: First, arrange with Walters to strain a quart of milk on Sat. morning, so that we can get it Sat. afternoon, and beginning Sunday take our usual two quarts a day again. Also for them to reserve a dozen eggs for us, to be called for Sat. afternoon. Second, will you please buy for us a 3 lb. roast of beef from the butcher on Sat. morning, one with plenty of fat to it preferred. Third, ask Clarence to reserve two loaves of bread for us--this as a precaution, so they won't be sold out by the time we arrive. Pardon me for taking this liberty and putting you to this trouble.

The meeting here is going along fine--close Sunday night --the tenth of this trip! Both of us are feeling O.K. & trust you & yours are ditto.

With best wishes,
Affectionately,
AWP

======================================

Herendeen note - AWP & wife arrived home 10/30/20
Remained in this area till January 1921--then to Calif. again.

======================================

20 Ministering Again in the Tent in Oakland to Smaller Crowds

596 22nd St., Oakland
Monday A.M. January 17th 1921

Mr. I.C. Herendeen
Beloved Bro. in the Lord:

We duly arrived here Thurs. A.M. at 8:40, very weary from our long journey. We came on the Burlington line from Chicago, and on the Rio Grande from Denver to Ogden. This took us over high altitudes, varying from 7,000 to 10,000 feet. We both of us found it very trying and were glad to get here.

You will want to know something of the conditions here. Well, the Devil has gotten in quite a little work since I left. It is the old story--jealousy. Bro. Ironside returned to Oakland in October to spend the winter here, and started a series of Bible readings in the Brethren Assembly Hall: but the people would not come to hear him--preferred Bro T. at the Tent. This incensed Bro. Ironside. Thompson took pity on him, and invited him to the Tent, but as soon as Ironside began crowds fell off markedly. The thing came to an issue one night when Bro. Ironside told the crowd from the platform of Bro. Thompson's Tent, that "all Bro. Thompson's talk of walking by faith, trusting the Lord etc., was so many idle words, that the assembly was behind Bro. Thompson, supporting him etc.!!" This, of course, was not true tho the Assembly had had quite a little fellowship with Bro. Thompson. After Ironside was through, Bro. Thompson arose and contradicted him to his face, and I gather there was quite a scene, Ironside getting very hot. A very short time after this, someone went round to see Bro. Ironside about Reprobation, taking him a marked copy of my book. Ironside seized on this and made the most possible out of it: said it was a bottle of deadly poison and so on: he warned all who belonged to the Assembly to burn my books & urged them to shun the Tent: most of the

Assembly folk have done so, and quite a few of the young converts have been so stumbled by the breach between Ironside and Thompson. They have gone back to their Demons disgusted with Brethrenism. But distressing as all this is, the Divine purpose in it is apparent: God invariably tests those who have professed to receive His truth.

On January 1st a huge Interdenominational Evangelistic Campaign was inaugurated in Oakland. Fourteen churches united, and erected a wooden tabernacle seating 5,000, with a most elaborate organ. Mr. John Brown, one of the best known Evangelists of the west, is here for a month--he knows quite a little truth, but is very chary in giving it out: he is 'on the fence', trying to please everybody--the one objective getting people to join the Church. The pastors have all given up their own services, excepting the Sunday morning service, and are constantly urging their members to be loyal and attend the Tabernacle. Thompson says, the whole campaign is a united, organized effort to starve him out: so there are "many adversaries." However, neither of us are at all discouraged--The Lord is testing our faith. When I got here, the attendance at the Tent had dwindled down to about 300 a night, with 500 Saturdays and Sundays. But they are already picking up some. Saturday night we had fully 500, Sunday afternoon same, and last night 700. I am having great liberty in ministering the Word, and am sure God is with us.

In addition to the other competitive movements, the Open Bible here are working a special effort at the present time to hold their people together (& keep them away from the Tent), and they, too, have provided a special attraction, and have secured an Evangelist for a week or 2 week meeting, and hold your breath when I tell you who it is--Alesor Marshall!! It is only to be expected that he will do all he can to fan the flame of opposition against my book--but God is over all: they can do nothing against the truth.

Bro. Thompson and I believe that in February, when all the counter meetings will be over, that the crowd will flock back to the Tent in even greater numbers. Already 20 or 30 of the "B" [Brethren?] have come out to hear me! Same have told Thompson I am just bursting to preach on

Reprobation, but thus far I have felt led to preach little but the simple Gospel. February 1st I expect to start in John's Gospel. Thompson stands firm with me on Sovereignty, excepting Reprobation where he wobbles a bit--pray for him regarding this. Weather is very wet and windy here just now, so God is sure testing His own from every point.

I return Mrs. Corey's letter--thanks for it. Also have endorsed cheque for $7.50 which please place to my a/c. Please send me some gummers in your next. No more now. Best wishes to "you all", & also kind regards to the Burds.

Cordially, Yrs. by Grace,
Arthur W. Pink

21 Larger Crowds in Oakland

596 22nd Street
Oakland, Cal.

Mr. I.C. Herendeen — January 18th 1921
Beloved Bro. in the Lord:

Thanks for the forwarded letters: I enclose check for $1.50 and M.O. [money order] for $4.10 which please place to my credit. The 50 copies of Millennium and 50 of Satan I have not placed on sale here yet: am waiting till Brown's meeting is over here, when I expect our crowds will double: I want you please to charge these to me at the 25% discount, and to allow me for what the Express charges on them would have been. Will you please send me three complete sets of my writings to above address, as I want to have them in exhibition in the Tent to take orders from later.

Will you please order for me "The Berean Exp" in <u>cloth</u> for 1920 and ask them, if they can, to send along an extra cover of the binding, for the one year I have the loose copies of.

The Lord gave me a glorious meeting last night: fully 500 out. Am still in Hebrews 11.

I went in Book Room here yesterday to get my mail: Mr. Crain was pleasant, but obviously ill at ease: said nothing tho regarding Sovereignty. Bro. I. was in his office--only glass partition between, but took no notice of me. They are afraid!

Weather conditions very wet and squally, but the people here in California are used to it, and it makes little difference to the attendances.

Prayed for you last Sunday morning: trust you had good time. Alesor Marshall has not shown up around the tent: is he afraid too?

I hear J.H. Stearnes has left Frisco for good--the work there being, comparatively a failure--and has gone, with his children, to New York. Poor Frisco! It seems abandoned by God.

There is much un-employment here as in most of the cities I imagine. Business very depressed. Sugar here 12 lbs. for a $1.00, prunes $.08 lb. but most other things [unclear word] than in Pa.

Best wishes from us both,
Yours by Grace,
Arthur W. Pink

22 A Discussion on God's Sovereignty in Salvation

596 22nd St., Oakland
January 21st, 1921

Dear Bro. Herendeen:

This time I have some news which I know will interest you. Tuesday night Bro. Thompson told me that Mr. Alesor Marshall had had a short talk with him that afternoon and was anxious to meet me, the three together. Bro. Thompson appointed a time for 2 yesterday afternoon. Bro. Marshall and I were there on time, but Thompson was 15 minutes late. Bro. Marshall was quite agreeable and for 10 minutes we discussed common places. He was not at ease and seemed to wait on me for an opening to introduce what I knew was uppermost in his mind. He had handed me a tract by Bennett on "Fellowship". So I gave him the opening thus. Said I, "I like Mr. Bennett's writings for he is more Calvinistic than most of the 'B' [Brethren?] writers"! Mr. Marshall replied, "Yes, but he would not go nearly so far as you go." At this time Bro. Thompson joined us. Our conversation lasted about 90 minutes, Mr. Marshall monopolized the conversation and as he is so much older than I, I refused to be rude and butt in 'too much'. Mr. Marshall's main point was based on I Tim 2:1-6. He pressed me as to the scope of the "all men" we are to pray for. I said "All without disfavor, not all without exception." He replied, "Bullingerism!" I said, No; the Scriptures warrant and necessitate such a distinction. I pinned him down then, and finally he allowed that in a few instances, "all men" is used in the N.T. in a restricted sense. He next pressed me for a reason for limiting "all men" in I Tim. 2:1--he said, "You have no reason: it's just your theories which demand it." I said, "Pardon me, but the example of my Lord warrants it"--He "prayed not for the world." We next had a long argument on that: Mr. Marshall insisting I had no right to appeal to John 17:9. He asked me what Christ was praying about there: and before I could answer said, "For the oneness of His own people, and hence he could not pray for 'the world' in such a connection." I challenged that: pointed out Christ was praying for other things beside the Unity of His people--among other things, for the salvation of those who should yet believe. Mr. Marshall tried hard to hold his point. Finally, I defied him by asking him to give me just one scripture anywhere else where Christ prayed for anyone else save His people! He next returned to I Tim 2 and pressed me hard on 2b. His main point was this: God had commanded us to preach the Gospel to every creature: if Christ died for the elect only, God is tantalizing non-elect sinners with an offer of salvation. On this point we first had a lengthy duel on whether or not the Gospel is an "offer"; ultimately he agreed it was not. Then he returned to his argument about "tantalizing" and we got nowhere on that point. Next he switched to John 3:16 and I first reminded him of C.E. Stuart's words on it, and he said--"Yes, sad indeed; Stuart was a hyper-C [Calvinist]". Then I said, "Wm. Kelly took the same view." And he said, "Yes, I know, & Mr. K. was another C [Calvinist]." I could not resist the temptation to say--I'm glad there has been one or two Calvinists even among the Brethren! We had it up and down on John 3:16, but, of course, neither convinced the other. He sighed & groaned, and kept saying, "now you see where Mr. Pink stands"--this to Bro. Thompson. He reserved his 'trump card' for the close. He said, "You believe God foreordained everything which comes to pass." I said, Yes. He said, "Some Christians have told lies, other have stolen: did God foreordain their sins? I said, "Certainly just as He did that Judas should betray Christ, and Israel crucify Him." He said, "Shocking, shocking", and Bro. Thompson groaned too. Mr. Marshall then closed his Bible and said "Further conversation is useless." The meeting thus terminated. But we shook hands and parted friendly. I was curious to see how Bro. Thompson was affected, but after the evening meeting, when we had a few minutes together, he made no reference to it, and seemed quite as usual toward me. We had a glorious meeting last night too! Attendances are steadily improving: about 800 out last night.

In our spare (small) room, on the top in the big box in which we have chunks of wood and paper, you will find a copy of Haldeman on Romans. Will you please forward this to Pastor L.M. Winstead, Madisonville, Ky., & charge postage to my account. No further news. Both of us are well, and trust "you all" are ditto. With best wishes,

Yrs by Grace
AWP

P.S. I rely on you treating as strictly confidential what I have recorded of conversation with Alesor M!

P.P.S. Will you please forward me, from time to time, my copies of "Our Hope," the "Wonderful Word", and "News & Truths." If the last mentioned has ceased coming, will you kindly send to HBT $1.50 for renewal & charge to my a/c.

23 A Long News-filled Letter

596 22nd Street
Oakland, Cal.
January 30th, 1921

Sunday morning
Beloved Brother in the Lord:

Your long looked for letter arrived yesterday--the first received from you! Was glad to hear of your meeting with Bro. Dean and of the opportunity the Lord gave you in prayer that the Holy Spirit will quicken him into all truth.

You asked me to keep you posted re developments here respecting the opposition. There has been little change since last I wrote. Neither Bro. I. [Ironside?] or Crain ever came near the Tent: they are scarcely civil when we go to the Book Concern for anything. Bro. I. is the "pope" of the Assembly, and has succeeded in persuading about two-thirds of its members to keep away from the Tent. But while, of course, this is deplorable, we are not greatly concerned: we are far more anxious to reach those of the Lord's people who are starving in the Denominations than we are to preach to those who (think they) know as much or more than we do--I mean "The B [Brethren?]." The meetings of Evangelist Brown at the Tabernacle close tonight, so another week should give us a better idea of what to expect in our Tent. Numbers of people who heard me regularly last September, have been out to the Tent once or twice this time, and have told me that as soon as Mr. Brown's meetings were over, they expected to hear me regularly. They feel obliged to attend the Tabernacle while Mr. Brown is here. They are most of them members of churches here, and have been praying for weeks past for these special Union meetings, and now that Mr. Brown is here, at the request of the churches, they feel duty bound to support him. Considering everything, the attendances at the Tent have been good: I believe I am within the mark when I say our average for the week night services this last two weeks has been between 600 and 700. Those who have come have been in earnest, and we have had some splendid times together. I gave seven addresses last week on Matthew's Gospel, dealing mainly with its Displ. [Dispensational] scope. One illustration which has come to my notice will show God is working. A Miss Owen who attends regularly, came to our rooms last Thursday morning quite excited. She desired me to accompany here to her flat at once. A nurse (about 40) had a room in Miss Owen's flat, had been there for three months. This nurse had been reared an Episcopalian, but now a member of Theosophy Society. Miss Owen (a very cultured and refined woman) had spoken a word to this nurse as opportunity provided, without forcing an opening, and had frequently invited her to the Tent. The nurse came out to hear me for the 1st time two weeks ago tonight, when I preached from Mark 16:16 dwelling much on "he that believeth not shall be damned." Miss Owen said the nurse returned home highly indignant and amazed that an intelligent man would preach such antiquated thought. Miss Owen left her alone, but prayed for her. Last Wednesday the nurse sought out Miss Owen and said I'm leaving tomorrow to spend the night with a friend in Berkeley, and Fri. A.M. I sail for Honolulu, & before I leave I want to hear Mr. Pink again!! Miss Owen was indisposed & could not go to the Tent Wed. night but the nurse came on alone!! I was speaking on Matt 8 and dwelt almost entirely on the Dispensational meaning & application of the miracles recorded therein, touching only briefly on the personal application. There was little or nothing in the address which I would have thought would affect a sinner. But the nurse returned home that night "all broken up", "deeply stirred" to use Owen's words. It was just the power of the Word, without man's comment on it!! Miss Owen said the nurse slept little Wed. night, & was still much affected Thurs. morning. Miss Owen told her I had been in Theosophy & asked her if she would like to have a talk with me. She said she would. So, Miss Owen came round & asked me to come right back as the nurse was leaving at 2:30 that afternoon for her friend in Berkeley. I went, but without an atom of faith! I felt it would be perfectly useless as my past experience in speaking with Theosophy had shown me you might as well talk to trees. But God was working, & in a "mysterious" way. I think I told you that there is an elderly Presbyterian preacher here who owns a complete set of "Things to Come" (Bullinger's) & had offered to loan them to me. I secured the first volume last Sunday & read it last week. In that very volume were some striking articles on "Theosophy" showing how it was opposed to Christianity. One article quoted from an address given by Mrs. Bessant in India, in which she contrasted Christianity with Buddhism (to curry favor with the Brahmin's!) & said the one was like colored glass over against a beautiful pearl. It also went on to say, Mrs. Bessant had entered a Buddhist temple barefooted, & had bowed to the idols. I took this volume along with me as I went to interview the nurse. When I got there she had composed herself, & sought shelter behind a mask of intellectual complacency & superiority. At her request, I discussed the fundamental tenets of Theosophy, & explained why I had left the Theosophy Society. She referred to some of their books & how they helped to explain (?) the Bible to her--this is their favorite bait for catching those in Christian countries "who don't know their Bibles". I got her to read the article in "Things to Come" & she was horrified when she discovered what Mrs. Bessant taught in the Theosophy headquarters in India. I was with her 3 hours. I left feeling I had made little impression on her except I had exposed their anti-Holy. To my surprise she was out at the Tent again that night. Friday Miss Owen phoned me to say, the Nurse had called on her early that morning, ere sailing for Honolulu, & handed to Miss Owen all her Theosophy books saying "I am thro with them forever." "But, O, Miss Owen pray for me, for I don't understand what salvation by the blood means"! Miss Owen gave her C.H.M.'s [C.H. Mackintosh] notes on Leviticus, and she left. We are praying God may bring her out of darkness into his marvelous light.

Now for your queries, Bro. Thompson has given away all the literature he got from you, excepting the Bibles. I have not heard him refer to the Concordance. He is going to see Mr. Crain about the books of mine he never got--will let you know outcome later, DV. Thanks for ordering "Berean Exposition".

We trust Bro. Clarence is better by this, shall pray for him.

Am sorry to read what you say re [regarding] new Edition of Sovereignty. I strongly urge you to seek quotation from other Binders. I am sure you can beat 50 cents today. Don't be stubborn, dear Bro: but write at once for quotations from other firms. My own impression as I write is--don't be in too big a hurry: I believe the paper market will collapse soon.

Yes, I shall try again for Clergy permit.

Weather here is very wet, with five spells of 2 or 3 days duration in between.

Alesor Marshall preached at the Tent last night: preaches tonight, Monday & Tuesday for open B [Brethren] here and leaves Wednesday for Los Angeles. His address last night was exceedingly poor: took as his text Rev. 3:21--Christ knocking at door of sinner's heart: latch on the inside, only the sinner could open it!! He quoted from 14 hymns and gave 15 anecdotes!! Nothing whatever for the Christian. He rang the charges again on John 3:16--"world" means "everybody"--"You, me and all others"--but he offered no proof for his assertion.

Must close now. Write again soon: tell us how you folks are. Glad to say both of us are OK.

Best wishes,
Yrs by Grace
A.W. Pink

24 Still in the Tent in Oakland

596 22nd Street, Oakland, Cal.
February 3rd, 1921

Beloved Brother in the Lord:

Thanks for the package of magazines to hand yesterday --not had time yet to go through them. The three sets of books which I ordered more than two weeks ago have not yet arrived: I don't understand this. I want to begin taking orders. Please advise me in plenty of time when I must cease including Sovereignty in the sets, also what the sets minus Sovereignty will be--will they be $4.25. Thanks for mailing Haldane to Winstead.

We have had considerable rain here the past two weeks, & a good deal of wind--they say unusually wet for these parts--it has been quite cool, but not cold. We look now for fine bright weather.

Industrial conditions are very bad here: 1000's out of employment: 100's of men lounging on the streets.

There is considerable sickness--colds, etc., and this is affecting attendances at the Tent. Our nightly average is six to seven hundred. But the interest is keen, & God's blessing manifest. Started in John's Gospel last night, Tuesday night spoke on Luke's Gospel--the Son of Man--emphasizing uniqueness of Christ's humanity. A man of about 50, quite cultured, told me at close of service, he was a regular church goer, & yet this was the 1st time in his life he had ever heard that Christ's flesh was different from ours! Is not the ignorance and lack of teaching deplorable?

Bro. Thompson has received another urgent call to come to Seattle: he thinks he will very likely leave here Feb 15 for 6 weeks and leave me in charge, and for him to return about the 1st week in April and for me to go on to Seattle alone and spend perhaps a couple of months there: he to return to continue the work here. We are praying over this.

We are going out to lunch; Mrs. P. is about ready, so I must quit. We both are keeping well, trust you all are ditto.

Cordially, Yrs. by Grace,
A.W. Pink

P.S. Tell me in your next how the Cowles matter is progressing.

25 A Description of the Services in the Tent

596 22nd St., Oakland
February 8/21

Beloved Brother in the Lord:

Yours of the 2nd to hand last night: sorry you never read my post card on which I ordered 3 sets of my writings. I certainly mailed it, 7 or 8 days after I got here. However, "all" things work together for good" so, doubtless, God has some purpose in allowing it to go astray. I hope, tho, the other sets, 7 or 10 will get here soon, as I am receiving quite a few inquiries. Could have sold half a dozen sets already had I had them here.

Yes, I was expecting those two books from Pasadena: you will find both are worth reading, tho the writer on Ephesians is rather "mixed up" on some things. By the way, have you received a little package from Bro. Daniels of Camilla, [state is unclear, being either La or Ga or Ca], addressed to me? If so, will you kindly forward it to me here, and much obliged.

Our nightly service is about thus: 7 P.M. prayer meeting for men only: I believe about 1/2 a dozen attend. 7:30 song service during which the crowd straggles in: usually Bro. Thompson is on the platform during this, and gives a 3 to 5 minute talk between hymns--his talk following the line of the last hymn; he is at his best here: very original, but nothing vulgar or cheap: 7:50 I arrive and go on platform: one more hymn, a prayer led by Bro. Thompson, brief announcements and at 8 sharp I begin speaking and continue till 9:15 or 9:20 and close in prayer. I am now expounding John 1. Occasionally someone in audience asks if he may put a question to which I say, Yes, if relevant--in nearly every instance it is eager souls seeking light. The ignorance is appalling: last night someone sent in a written request (in an educated hand)--How could John have written the 4th Gospel seeing he was beheaded by Herod before Christ's death?!! At the close of the service when I had spoken on Luke's presentation of Christ as the Son of Man: a man of considerable culture, 45 to 50 years old, came to me and said, I've been attending churches all my life, but this is the 1st time I have ever heard Christ's humanity was different from ours!! Last night one of the younger "B" [Brethren] who minsters the Word--an intimate friend of Bro. I. [Ironside?]--was out. After my exposition of John 1:13 he called out, may I put a question: I said, Yes, if it is pertinent. He said, You've just told us the new birth is due solely to the mighty working of God in us--Does God work thus upon all? I replied, No, certainly not. He then said, May I ask another question--I said, What is your object--to seek light, or start an argument? He said--Light. I said, Go ahead: "Then are those who are not born again damned because God did not work so mightily in them as in those who believe?" I said, No--they are damned because they have consciously and deliberately rejected Christ. No doubt he expected a different answer--the one from the Div [Divine] side. I believe he was "primed" beforehand.

Now for your queries: Yes, the opposition meetings ended January 31. No; our attendances are not increasing: for one thing Bro. I. [Ironside?] and members of his association are working hard warning everyone they know against us at the Tent. But the main thing has been the weather--not really bad, but very uncertain and unsettled: about every 3rd day is cold and raining and others threaten to be; then, too there is considerable sickness about. Our nightly average is around 600 to 650 to 700. Bro. Thompson is exceedingly cordial toward me: not the slightest friction at any time: we understand each other and allow for eccentricities. Most, almost all of the tracts you sent him are disposed of. I shall urge him tomorrow, DV, to send you a check--he is very un-businesslike.

I enclose 2 letters from ACG [A.C. Gabelein] (please return them in due course)--they show how friendly disposed he is toward me. Note what he says re [regarding] book at "under 1.50"! I fear if you get 1000 Sovereignties at $1.75 retail you will have little demand later on--books etc are bound to drop with other things.

Am very crowded--studying hard, etc. Sent ACG [A.C. Gabelein] "Gen" [Genesis] article today.

Both of us are quite well and trust you all are ditto--hope the "all" won't increase again this time during our absence.

Continue praying for us, as we shall for you.

Love in Christ,
AWP

P.S. Is not the enclosed [word unclear] terrible--[word unclear], or burn it!

26 Conflict with Other Believers in Oakland

596 22nd Street, Oakland, Cal. February 14th, 1921

Beloved Brother in the Lord:

I am feeling rather "Mondayish" this A.M. but want to send you a few lines. The opposition continues hot and strong, but God is on the throne. The majority of the Christian folks are mad because Bro. Thompson continued his meetings during the time Evangelist Brown was here:

several of the leading ministers had called on Bro. Thompson before Brown came and requested him to close down: then Brown's own "advance agent" called on him and renewed the request. But he declined: said there was plenty of room and need for both: that they would not conflict, inasmuch as Brown's would be evangelistic and his own teaching for Believers. Of course, this incensed them. They regarded my coming here just at the time I did as a "plot"--an extra effort on the part of Bro. Thompson to draw people away from Brown's meetings. In consequence, not a few of the Ch [Church] folks have "got the hump" & won't come near the Tent. Those in the Ironside Asst [Association] are afraid to come: most of those of the "Open B" [Brethren] have ceased coming since Alesor Marshall was here. But, notwithstanding, God is at work--a good opportunity for Him to show His hand!! Last week we averaged around 500. Those who come are in earnest and are being blessed. Saturday night Bro. Thompson preached: 700 out. Yesterday we had two glorious meetings: 800 in afternoon, and almost 1000 at night. The Lord gave me much liberty. Bro. Thompson leaves this week for Seattle: expects to be away 3 weeks. A Presbyterian Bro. will preach for me, DV, Saturday evenings.

Mrs. Rita Dooling was here Saturday night and she says she never received her set of books! Address was c/o General Delivery, Richmond, California. Will you send out a searcher or tracer right away, and let me know as soon as you hear.

Please send 500 "Not Saved" to Mr. Robert A. Painter, 593 Sycamore St., Oakland, California. Charge to me: I do not want any discount or royalty on this. Kindly let me know price: I priced them to him at $3.00 but was not sure this was correct.

Weather much better, some warmer, this last week: but occasional rains still. Both of us are well. Best wishes,

Yrs. by Grace
AWP

27 An Apparent Indication They Are to Stay in Ministry in Oakland

721 16th Street
Oakland
February 23rd/21

Beloved Brother in the Lord:

Since last I wrote things have improved, generally speaking. Quite a number have come to me, spontaneously, telling of how much help and blessing they have received from the Bible Expositions: all last week the Lord granted me signal joy and liberty in ministering His Word. Sunday night a 1000 were out, & I spoke on Zaccheus: many were deeply stirred. Then, the sale of the books has improved, as no doubt you deduced from the order on the back of my last envelope. Further, the monetary gifts have been more frequent, & we have now received a little above our expenses in getting out here. The opposition is still fierce, but this is to be expected, of course. Mr. Ironside has ceased speaking only once a week at the Gos. Aud. [Gospel Auditorium] here and this week begins to speak three times a week, on the book of Zechariah. He has also gotten out cards announcing the meetings, and urging all lovers of the Word to attend. He is finding it hard to hold his crowd.

Something happened on Monday that deeply impressed us both, and seems to indicate the Lord intends us to remain here some time. A lady (whom neither of us knew) sent a note asking Vera to call her up. This lady owns a large apartment house, of the better class, divided off into suites of 4 rooms each. She said she had a suite vacant and felt strongly the Lord wanted us to have it. Decent rooms are hard to get: the one we occupied in 22nd St., was respectable, and quiet, with a 3 burner gas stove, fitted up for light housekeeping--but unsuited, of course, to receive visitors in, and often some of the ladies wanted to call on Mrs. Pink. We were paying $6.00 a week for it! This is the regular price for a room fitted up to do light housekeeping in. I felt impressed by what Vera had learned over the phone, so the two of us went almost right away to look over the suite. We found it, considerably above expectations: almost brand new: fully furnished. A front room with 3 windows with a bed that swings back to the wall, with a mirror in front, so that when not in use it looks like a wardrobe. A dining room, with a nice writing desk in it: a kitchenette, and a private bathroom. Everything in it we need--dishes, linen, silverware to be all furnished with the rooms. The owner told us her husband came frequently to the tent, and both of them were Christians--Kentucky Baptists! She said the Lord had definitely laid it on her heart to offer us the suite at the same price we were paying for our one room, $6.00 per week. We gratefully and gladly accepted her offer and moved in that same evening. We are delighted with our new quarters and thankful to our God for such gracious provision. So, I say, it looks as tho He meant for us to stay awhile longer.

Bro. Thompson is now in Seattle--have not heard from him.

I enclose cheques for $50.00 (fifty dollars) which please place to my a/c. Kindly furnish me with a statement showing how much the 50 "Satans" and 50 "Millenniums" were, also the total amount of the last lot I ordered, with the balance owing you after this $50 is deducted, and obliged.

Weather is much warmer this last few days. Went with a Brother for a 12 mile "hike" in the hills yesterday--enjoyed it immensely. Both of us are feeling fine. Trust you are ditto. Best wishes.

Yrs by Grace,
AWP

How is your Brother in Los Angeles getting along now? Please send me some more gummers.

28 Opposition from a Well-known Christian Leader

721 16th Street
Oakland, Calif.
Feb. 28, 1921

Dear Bro. Herendeen:

Mr. Pink has gone across the bay to San Francisco to spend the day with Mr. John Stearnes. He had to rush so did not have time to write you and I told him I would send a few lines for him.

The meetings are still very encouraging. They are well attended and there is a real interest in the study of the Word on the part of those who do come. Last night there was almost 1000 again. <u>But</u> when God's Word prospers the enemy gets busy and does everything in his evil power to counteract the good. The opposition is getting stronger and stronger on the part of Mr. Ironside. He took it upon himself to write Bro. A.C.G. [A.C. Gabelein] a letter, when he heard that he promised to come to the tent for 3 days in April, telling him that Mr. Pink was teaching "damnable heresy," that he said publicly "the way to hell is paved with babies," and further said A.C.G. was doing a great wrong to publish "Gleanings in Genesis" in "Our Hope" and advised him strongly to cease having them printed. Personally, we feel Bro. G. [Gabelein] has too much sense to listen to H.A.I. [H.A. Ironside] for he knows that those articles of Arthur's have brought in innumerable subscriptions for the O.H. ["Our Hope"].

It is pathetic how much jealousy there is among Bible teachers. He [H.A. Ironside?] had a man at the tent door last night, with his car, asking those who were going in the tent to come with him to the Gospel Auditorium for there was just as good teaching there. I don't know how many he took away but I do know some came to me and said "when they asked me to go there, I replied, No indeed, I am going in here."

Well, I have told you enough blue and gloomy things for one letter. Amid it all, we are happy because we know they can do nothing against the truth. God's Word is being taught and nothing else so we leave it all to Him. It only shows us that all are still human and some are letting the old nature get the best of them. We are not sure yet how much longer we will be here but I believe until end of March anyway.

Bro. Thompson is in Seattle yet and does not know when he will return. It is a chance he has not sent you a check before now. Arthur told him twice to do so and he said he would. We will get after him again D.V.

Last night I got an order for a concordance. The gentleman wants one just like Arthur's. Send it to us here as soon as you can & charge to Arthur.

Also 50 "Way of Salvation" A.W. P. [A.W. Pink].

The 10 sets you sent are gone and I am waiting for the others.

My letter is getting long so I must close. Remember me to Mrs. H. [Herendeen].

With Christian greetings. I remain,

Sincerely,

(Mrs.) Vera Pink
721 16th Street, Oakland
March 2nd, 1921

29 Opposition Continuing and Words concerning the Second Edition of the Sovereignty Book

Mr. I.C. Herendeen
Beloved Brother in the Lord:

Yours of the 21st and 24th duly to hand with best thanks. You say "Am enclosing Mr. M's letter," and in postscript add, decided not to send it. Was it a letter from

Mr. Mauro? I conclude it was, and imagine that he wrote to say he was glad you had now decided to meet Mrs. C's [Cowles] lawful (?) claims, but regretted you had been so tardy too. Am I right? Thanks for returning ACG's [A.C. Gabelein's] letters.

I rejoice with you that the trouble with Mrs. C [Cowles] is now closed--for all time I trust. I have praised the Lord for this issue and I begged Him to deal mercifully with her.

Also very glad to hear what you say re [regarding] prices on the binding of the new Edition of "Sovereignty". We have prayed much over this. Last night between 11 PM and 1 AM, I carefully re-read the whole of the manuscript on the new material for this book. I am deeply thankful for the gracious aid God granted me in the "composition". I feel strongly led to add one more appendix, if it is at all possible to get it in in time, which I hope will prove the case. In my stay here I find that one of the points which most trouble the Lord's own people is the limiting of the term "world" in John 3:16. I have therefore given much prayerful study to this verse, and last night composed and this AM have written out some new thoughts upon it. I enclose same. I am certain it will help many, and simplify the seeming difficulty. Try your best, dear bro., to get this in. Have the printers insert a note at the foot of p. 193 (in the original Edition) --the X (paragraph) coming at the end of first paragraph on p. 193 after "pious sentimentalist"--the footnote to read:--

See appendix 3 on "Kosmos." Let appendix 3 be added at foot of "Table of Contents" too, please.

Glad to know the other things I ordered have been started--the 10 sets arrived O.K.

The opposition here is very fierce: last Friday night (when Mr. Ironside was giving an address on Zechariah) and also on Sunday night, two of "the Brethren" in fellowship at the Gospel Auditorium stood outside the Tent, when the crowd was gathering and intercepted those they knew and urged them not to enter the Tent, but go with them to hear Mr. I. [Ironside] at the Aud. offering to convey them out there in their autos!! This does not "move" us, but it shows their animosities. I learned last week that Mr. I. [Ironside] had written to A.C.G. [A.C. Gabelein] telling him

I was teaching the most damnable heresies here, including the Damnation of Infants, and urging him not to publish any more of my articles in "Our Hope". One of the Auditorium sisters told Mrs. Thompson, A.C.G. [A.C. Gabelein] had replied saying if what he had written was true, he (ACG) would cease publishing my articles, having any further fellowship with me, and would refuse to speak on the same platform; adding he was going to write me. Thus far I have not heard anything on this from ACG--will let you know about it if I do. But not withstanding the opposition, the attendances are being maintained, many are being blessed and God's blessing is very manifest. I have now spent over 50 hours on John's gospel, and am only 1/2 way thro Chapter 4! You can imagine how minutely I am going thro it, and the close study this involves!

Had a letter yesterday from Mrs. Barbour: she says Mr. B. [Barbour] is teaching the class, and they have been on Romans for the last 2 months or so: last week Mr. B. [Barbour] expounded Chapter 9 and there was a "rumpus"!! Several said they were thro with the class: thus God's Word "sifts" everywhere!

Had a letter from Bro. Cole of Morton Gap asking me to come to the Institute for a week in April. But I cannot. I feel God will keep me here some time yet: how long I don't know.

Please place enclosed check of $2.15 to my a/c [account].

Must stop now. Both of us are quite well. Weather lovely this past week.

Hurriedly but Cordially,
Yrs by Grace,
AWP

P.S. Have not had time to examine carefully Trench's book on "After the [words unclear]".

30 Book Sales and Sermon Topics

721 16th Street
Oakland, Calif.
March 7th, 1921

Mr. I.C. Herendeen
Beloved Brother in the Lord:

Yours of the 28th ult. duly to hand. The enclosed statement tallies with what I had calculated: showing a balance owing you of $37.13, since which I have remitted a check for $2.15 leaving present balance of $34.98. I hope to remit this within about a week, DV.

Kindly fill the following order as quickly as possible: six complete sets--charge to me.

50 the "Death of Christ" (pamphlet, giving Introduction to 7 Sayings)
50 "The Divine Inspiration"--pamphlet - giving substance of chapter from the book
200 "The Wrath of God"
250 "The Way of Salvation"
200 "Your Correct Weight".

Make out these five items on bill to Mr. Robt. A. Painter, 593 Sycamore, Oakland, but send the package containing same addressed direct to me: also please send bill for same to me, and I will, DV, collect for you and forward. I do not desire any discount for myself on Bro. Painter's order, but if you feel disposed to you might make a small discount at the foot of Bro. Painter's bill--he is a working man, and the tracts he will use for free distribution.

I note what you say regarding visiting the Chiropractor and shall pray that it may please the Lord to give efficacy to his efforts. Let me hear if you "get results."

Thank you for inspecting our house for possible leak.

Yes, Sunday night I depart from John's Gospel and address myself more especially to the Unsaved, dwelling almost entirely on man's ruin. So far I have spoken Sunday nights from Mark 16:16, Luke 13:23, the Prodigal Son, Blind Bartimeus, Zaccheus, and last night from Acts 17:30,31--The Judgment Day. About a 1000 out last night: had great liberty and a most solemn time: a number appeared to be deeply affected.

I have heard nothing yet from A.C.G.[A.C. Gabelein]. Bro. Thompson expects to be back from Seattle this week: have not heard how he fared there.

The meetings here offered much ground for praise: you are right: the present opening is "the opportunity of my life." Continue praying for us.

Cordially,
Yrs. by Grace,
A.W. Pink

P.S. Please enclose a few stickers in each of your letters.

31 Continuing Opposition and the Possibility of Going to Seattle with Brother Thompson

721 16th Street
Oakland, Cal.
March 12th, 1921

Mr. I.C. Herendeen
Beloved Brother in the Lord:

Your welcome letter of the 5th inst. to hand last night. Up to the time of writing I have heard no word from A.C.G. [A.C. Gabelein]. A man here of the name of Matlock and who is a member of H.A.I.'s [H.A. Ironside's] Assembly, is going around showing people a letter he claims to have received from A.C.G. [A.C. Gabelein] in an effort to prejudice people against me: many have told him to his face they have no wish to read it. Bro. Thompson, who has returned from Seattle, told me last night he intended to see this letter for himself and find out what was in it. I have had very little time with Bro. Thompson off the platform and know little more than when I last wrote: he is very cordial toward me, but rather more reticent than formerly. I gather, tho, he expects to go to Seattle, probably about the middle or end of April, and that he is anxious for me to accompany him when he leaves here.

I note what you say re the chiropractor, and only hope the results desired may be effected. But, I must say that personally I am very skeptical. In the first place, does it seem reasonable that no matter what may be the matter with a person the trouble can be righted by a few spinal adjustments? It makes no difference what a person may be suffering from, the chiropractor boasts that he can cure him--and everybody by the <u>same</u> method--pressure on the vertebra--that is too much for me to swallow.

Yes, now that the Cowles matter is settled, you must expect the old serpent to strike in some other direction, but thank God, he cannot strike except as the Most High permits.

I received another order last night: please fill the following, if still possible: 5 copies of "God's Sovereignty", and 5 copies of "Inspiration" in cloth--the new ones at $1.00.

I also enclose check for $35.00 payment of a/c rendered Feb. 28th, viz of $37.13--since which date I have forwarded you a check for $2.15 leaving a balance of $34.98--add 2 cents to it.

From now on will you please change the a/c from my name to my wife's. My reason for asking this is as follows: the Eastern Clergy Bureau refused to grant my Clergy Permit on the ground that I was not engaged <u>exclusively</u> in religious work: I was honest enough to tell them I sold my own books. I have therefore decided to remove this objection by letting Mrs. Pink do all the selling from now on: so in accordance with this I want the a/c to be in her name, please.

Also from now on, will you please forward to us a separate invoice for each lot ordered. On February 25 you charge me up with $26.37, but I believe, the amount positive, this was too little by about $2.00. If you can give me an itemized invoice of how this $26.37 was made up, I will compare it with Vera's list of what was received: it appears Victor sent too many of some of the booklets, tho am not sure.

Weather has been cloudy and cool all this week, and the attendance has been rather thinner, tho last night we had a good crowd out.

Both of us are in the best of health and trusting this will find you ditto, and the best wishes to you & C. & A. Burd,

I remain,
Yours by Grace,
A.W. Pink

P.S. Please add to the above order one dozen "Philosophy of Spiritualism" and one dozen "God of Jacob".

32 Displeasure over the Unbusiness-like Practices of His Associate

721 16th Street
Oakland, Cal.
March 18, 1921

Mr. I.C. Herendeen
Beloved Brother in the Lord:

Yours of the 12th inst, with enclosures, just to hand, with thanks. Bro. Thompson took lunch with us today and was here when your letter arrived. I asked him if he had sent you his check yet. He was rather surprised and embarrassed by the question. Said he had been so rushed of late, he had quite forgotten it. I criticized him sharply for his unbusiness like ways and for being so dilatory. He asked me to apologize to you for him and promised to send check tomorrow: I trust he will.

Bro. Thompson was quite elated over the fact that "Help and Food" is now publishing a report of the open Bible readings in the "Gospel Auditorium" here last September, on Roman 9 and 10 in which Bro. C. Crain was the main speaker and in which I took a small part, asking Bro. C.

[Crain] some pointed questions. Bro. Thompson says it is "pretty strong", almost as pointed as what I have been giving out at the Tent: rather surprised it has been published: thinking of getting a quantity to distribute in the Tent. Bro. Thompson is a "queer fish": one day he will come out quite strong regarding God's Sovereignty--in favor of it--but next day, criticizes me for "riding a hobby horse," etc. So about us leaving Oakland: one night he makes some remark in his announcements which leads the people to believe we shall remain indefinitely, probably all summer: next night he tells them we may leave at short notice, perhaps by the end of March: thus he has them guessing.

Am glad to hear what you say regarding "Sovereignty," and trust the binders will do their work well, and expeditiously. Will take no more orders in the meantime. As to the "R. R" [Redeemer's Return], I would like to go carefully thro it, and make a few alterations, and will get at this as soon as possible: the "7 sayings" I can think of no changes for it except a little thinner paper next time.

Weather here has been grand of late: little or no rain and quite a little warmer. Am having a "good time" in John: complete chapter 6 tonight, DV. I would like to stay here long enough to go right thro with it, but cannot tell whether I shall or not. The Lord has given me quite a little new light on a number of things in John: have not studied Romans any further since we left Swengel.

Please send us: one hundred "Not Saved" and ditto "Way of Salvation," one dozen "Mary"--also a few more "gummers". Trusting you are all well and with best wishes, I remain

Yours by Grace,

AWP

33 Business and Health Matters

721 16th Street
Oakland, Cal.
March 25, 1921

Beloved Brother in the Lord:

Your good letter of the 16th duly to hand: also the six sets, also Mr. Painter's order. Regarding the February 25th invoice: the numbers of the booklets check up alright. As to the prices--yes the four sets were overcharged 50 cents each, inasmuch as they included "Inspiration" of the 60 cent editions: where the new ones at $1.00 are put in the set will be $4.50, minus "Sov" $3.25. The reason I overlooked your overcharge was because I thought the 60 cent edition of "Insp" [Inspiration] was exhausted. Please credit Mrs. Pink's account with this $2.00. The demand for the literature here has dropped off lately. Pray with us the last lots you have sent will be disposed of.

On Monday I felt the first symptoms of a cold, and Tuesday felt as tho I was in for a case of the flu. Wednesday felt worse, so I decided to take some medicine: you know my style--no half measures. I have with me a bottle of tablets which I procured from Dr. Brown: they are very powerful and the bottle says "5 to 10 grains full dose." Dr. Brown told me if I ever took any to be sure and be very quiet the following day, as he only gave them to patients in bed. Tuesday night I took 15 grains and Wednesday morning 10 grains more. I took it quietly thro Wednesday but went and preached Wednesday night. Yesterday I felt "rotten"--head buzzed and heart felt as tho it was nearly out of commission. Was unable to get out and speak last night: felt groggy this morning: slept from noon till 2 and got up feeling much better. Expect to preach tonight. Anyway, my cold has gone--so what matters?

Am hoping new edition of Sovereignty will be out by end of April! As near as can now judge, Seattle by end of April.

Now two commissions for you: I want a book in my library which contains an article by JND [J.N. Darby] concerning the Human Will, but cannot remember name of the book. It is 1 of 3 which contain, each, 12 issues of a magazine published I believe in England about 1878. Brethren publication, I believe you have some 3 volumes, duplicated, on shelves in your office: these volumes contain various articles by C.G.S., J.N.D. [J.N Darby] etc. One has an article in it entitled "Should a Christian Fight?" I want you, please, to send me just the one which has in it Darby's article on the Will: send it as soon as possible.

Second, in revising the R.R. [Redeemer's Return], I would like to have some criticisms which my father sent me on this book 2 years ago: I preserved them, but am not sure just where they are: I believe you will find them, either on the small file of letters hanging on wall of little spare room, or else among the things I left on the dining table: they will not be in the boxes of sermons, but among the loose papers: you will be able to pick out my father's handwriting: there are 8 or 10 pages, about size of this one on thick, crackly, rice paper: kindly see if you can spot it on the table, if not, don't waste time searching--for if it is not on the table, I know not where it is, unless on the paper file.

With best wishes to all, and cordial greetings,

AWP

34 Evangelism at a Carnival near the Tent

721 16th Street
Oakland, Cal.
March 28, 1921

Beloved Brother in the Lord:

Three times last week, as also three times the week before, I asked Bro. Thompson if he had yet sent you his remittance: I was determined to keep on asking to shame him until he did: I reminded him several times of the text "Owe no man anything." He does not mean anything by it, but like many others is slack and careless. Well, I asked him again on Friday and he said "I have remitted..." I was glad to hear it: kindly let me know in your next whether he did so in full. Friday night a letter arrived from you for Bro. Thompson care of myself. I took it in my pocket to the Tent Saturday night, but forgot to hand it to him. The same thing recurred again yesterday. This a.m. it occurred to me there was probably nothing in it but a bill and request for payment. As Bro. Thompson had already remitted , I felt you would prefer for me not to hand him now your letter. So I took the liberty of opening it, and my conclusion was confirmed: I have destroyed it. Trust I did right and as you would have desired.

We had two splendid Meetings yesterday: it was a glorious day, brilliant sunshine throughout. Had about 600 out in the afternoon and 800 at night. I spoke both times on the Resurrection of Christians. God gave me much liberty and joy in delivering the messages.

On April 11th, a carnival is to come on the rear part of the lot on which Bro. Thompson's Tent is pitched--it's a very large lot. Two thirds of those who attend the carnival will have to pass right by the Tent. Bro. Thompson expects many will drop in the Tent. He plans to have Gospel services (twice a day, I believe) that week--it is to last only 6 days--and I think he intends to do all the preaching: at any rate, he announced yesterday the Studies in John's Gospel would be discontinued for that week. I want you to send me five thousand (5,000) of my leaflets on "Salvation" for distribution among those attending the carnival: please charge these to me direct: all other things to Mrs. Pink. By the way, we have received no invoice from you for the Concordance received 2 weeks ago; nor for the last six sets of my writings, to hand a week since!

Am hoping the new edition of Sovereignty will be out soon, tho I don't anticipate much demand for it here. Both of us are now in the best of health again--recovered from colds--trust you are all ditto. With best wishes,

Yours by Grace,
AWP

35 An Order for Books from Mrs. Pink

Dear Bro. Herendeen:

Please send me as quickly as possible 5 sets of Mr. Pink's writings minus Divine Inspiration, God's Sovereignty and also Satan and His Gospel (because I have plenty of these on hand). In addition please send 1 dozen each of Sins of S.[Saints], New Birth, and 3 fold. Put these on bill with concordance and other 6 sets.

Sincerely,

Mrs. Pink

36 An Open Door, It Seems, in Seattle

721 16th Street
Oakland, Cal.
April 7th, 1921

Beloved Brother in the Lord:

Your last two letters to hand with thanks. With reference to your query as to which issues of "Help & Food" contain accounts of the Bible readings here last September on Romans 9 & 10: January, February, March and April of this year. I have read the Feb & Mar ones only: they are reduced in size, and the wording has been carefully altered in several of Bro. Crain's statements. I understand H.A.I. [H.A. Ironside] "revised" them! Still I am surprised and pleased there is as much in them as there is. When ordering, please get copies of January and April for me and forward in due course.

We were rather surprised to get the news of Bro. Smith being married--poor Lucile! Wonder what sort of girl he has married, and what he expects to do.

Glad to hear you spoke straight to Vs. 5: am satisfied the poor fellow is off mentally.

No, I have not received a single word from A.C.G. [A.C. Gabelein]--"no news is good news"!

I spoke to Bro. Thompson about the balance he now owes you, and he understands. I believe he is rather "short" just now, but am not sure as he never says anything about finances--never once asked me how I am getting along since we arrived--his style is "happy-go-lucky". Thankful to say God has fully met our need.

Yesterday, Bro. Thompson received a wire from G. Whitney. Bro. Thompson told me after his return from Seattle that he had thoroughly looked over the ground there and that he picked out the best lot for his Tent when he should move there: a lot right in the very heart of the city, at the head of a triangle, with 3 of the most crowded thoroughfares skirting it. The lot was not to be obtained when he was there, but he made the owner an offer: Bro. Thompson told me "he had put it up to the Lord; that without God's help he could not expect to get the lot; that if God wanted him to move to S. to enable him to secure it." Yesterday wire came saying, "Lot can be secured: come at once: badly needed." So we expect to leave here by the end of this month, possibly by the 25th. Bro. Thompson is quite elated: he has wired Bro. Whitney to have the lot levelled right away, and is ordering a flat car from the Railway for his own Gospel car & tent. He is going to have a gallery built around the sides of Tent, to seat in all, 3,000: expects huge crowds in Seattle. Tells me I shall have the time of my life. Is willing for me to push sale of my literature there but wants me to shut out "Sov." I discount some of his big talk, but if half of his expectations are realized you can expect some big orders in another six weeks time--pray definitely about this: I count this more important than my oral ministry. God's blessing has been on the lit. here, heard of a cultured but godless Jewess but a few nights ago picked up a copy of "Millennium" from one who recently bought it, and she appeared to be deeply stirred and unusually interested, and requested something on prophecy and Salvation as we Gentiles see them: she got "Satan and his Gospel"!

Have taken 50 new subscriptions for "Our Hope" while here, so that ought to sweeten ACG [A.C. Gabelein]!

Continue addressing your letters to above address till I notify you. With best wishes,

Yrs. by Grace
AWP

37 Disappointment among the People in Oakland That He Is Going to Seattle

721 16th Street
Oakland, Cal.
April 11th, 1921

Beloved Brother in the Lord:

Yesterday we had two splendid services, the Tent being well filled: in the afternoon I spoke on John 13--Footwashing, and in the evening on the Lord's Return--John 14. As so many were anxious that I should get through John's Gospel before I left, I have been speeding up the last two weeks: giving but two addresses on each chapter: the week before last I spoke 7 times, and last week 8 times: have now given 77 addresses in all this trip. Last night's service was the best of them all: the Lord giving me unusual liberty. Today the "Carnival" commences on the rear of the lot on which Bro. Thompson's tent is pitched: there will be considerable noise and racket: expect many will drift into the Tent out of curiosity, stay a few minutes and leave. Bro. Thompson said "snappy and breezy talks" would be needed for such crowds. So I suggested he do this preaching--a type I am not cut out for.

Since the announcement was made that we expect to leave here by the end of April, a number of most interested ones here have expressed dismay at the thought of the meetings (now been running 11 months) should cease. Some have suggested buying the tent from Bro. Thompson and he to get a new one in Seattle: some want him to go on there and me remain here. But I do not feel this is of the

Lord. Bro. Thompson is very erratic: told the crowd yesterday "we were not gone yet: God could keep us here if He wanted to": asked the people to pray about it, and so on, and yet he has already wired Bro. Whitney to secure the lot in Seattle! He told me he thought it would be nice for us to divide forces, and he go to Seattle and me remain here, and later him return here and me go on to Seattle. I told him "nothing doing". When I am thro John, I believe God is thro with me here: also said, I had left the pastorate for this reason--not to confine myself to one place, but go from place to place, encouraging the saints and "strengthening the things which remain." I still expect we shall leave here by end of April and go on to Seattle but--cannot be certain, till we have actually started.

Glad to say the last 5 sets and also the "Salvation" tracts all arrived O.K. this morning: praise the Lord: thank you for your promptness of dispatch. The sets are already sold: so hope to take other orders. By the way, have you yet found out re Mrs. Dodan's lost set of last September?

Mrs. Pink encloses her check for $46.88 which according to your invoice balances a/c to the end of March. This amount is made up as follows:

March 9:	7.50	
March 12:	4.20	
March 12:	27.00	
March 16:	4.56	
March 23:	4.27	
March 23:	1.35	
	48.88	
Less -	2.00	- this amount overcharged by you on invoice of Feb 25, and overpaid by me in my check of $35.00 on Mar 12/21
	46.88	

Kindly let me know in your next if this $48.88 balances a/c to end of March.

According to invoices to hand, this leaves owing by me the 5,000 "Salvation" which please change to $15.00 as I do not desire any discount on these--these being for distribution, and $15.10 by Mrs. Pink for last invoice of April 4. D.V. each of us will send checks for these items within a few days. Please say in your next if all that is now outstanding against either of us (after you credit Mrs. Pink for enclosed $46.88) is the $15.00 to me and the $15.10 to Mrs. Pink.

Hoping to hear that the new edition is now in hands of binders, and trusting all is O.K. with you and yours. I remain,

Yrs by Grace,
AWP

38 A Congenial Word from A.C. Gabelein

721 16th Street
Oakland, Cal.
April 14th, 1921

Beloved Brother in the Lord:

I received last night a brief letter from ACG [A.C. Gabelein] in which he states he had just returned from California, telling me of the plans he is making for the Fall, and saying "I apprec. [appreciate] very much the subscriptions you have sent for 'Our Hope'." No reference at all to his letter to anything unpleasant!!

I enclose my check for $15.00 for the 5,000 "Salvation" leaflets.

Everything is going along smoothly here and as far as I know now we shall leave about the 25th. It is reported the weather in Seattle is now glorious: here been quite cold the last few days.

Please fill the following orders:

4 copies of the "Millennium" (enlarged edition) to Mr. R. Dybergh, 418 Southern Pacific Building, San Francisco
4 copies of R.R. [Redeemer's Return] to Miss M. Anderson, 407 29th Street, Oakland, and
1 copy of Insprn. [Inspiration] (cloth) to Mrs. Kingrea, 1935 E. 17th St., Oakland

Charge these to Mrs. Pink, please: also please transfer Mrs. Wessinger's order to Mrs. Pink's a/c and any similar ones that may come in.

Excuse more this time: best wishes,

AWP

39 Planning to Close in Oakland, Hoping to Go to Seattle, But Also Still Desiring to Write

721 16th Street
Oakland, Cal.
April 21/21

Beloved Brother in the Lord:

It is now practically certain we shall leave here early next week for Seattle. Bro. Whitney dropped in on us Sat. night last--he is here on a business trip around the Bay Cities. He told us, the friends in Seattle had secured the desired lot on which to pitch the Tent--right in the very heart of the city--and that they had already paid the rent on it for May and June. I suppose they did that to make sure of getting Bro. Thompson this time, he has disappointed them so often before. Bro. Thompson is very reluctant to close down the work here, and has tried hard to get people here to buy the tent from him (he has to get a new one in Seattle) and run it themselves, trusting the Lord to send them speakers, until the fall when he would probably return here from Seattle. But while a few favor this plan, the majority are sceptical--fearing the work would collapse after Bro. Thompson's departure as I believe it would. Then, there came along a

Bro. Pietsch on Sunday: he helped me in the meetings for two weeks while Bro. Thompson was in Seattle during March. Bro. Pietsch was a member of Ironside's assembly: but withdrew some two years ago, and now is a "free lance." He has been much of his time in Honolulu, but back in the country since January--spent a month in Gospel Auditorium in Seattle. there is not much to him as a speaker: an Evangelist, lacking the originality and personality of Bro. Thompson. But "made good" in Honolulu among the English speaking people there: has a sort of a combined mission and Bible Institute there. He expects to return late this fall: is very anxious that I should go there for a couple of months--Nov & Dec: guarantees me crowds of 500 to 1,000: says D. Evans (late of Chicago) had a 1000 every night for 3 weeks when he was there last fall: am praying over this. Well, Bro. Pietsch expects to be around the Bay here this summer, and Bro. Thompson has tried to sell the Tent here to him: Bro. Pietsch appears to be seriously considering this proposition, tho per [personally], I hardly think he will be busy. He is now out of the city and Bro. Thompson is exchanging wires with him daily. In case Bro. Pietsch buys, I expect we shall remain here thro most of next week, till he arrives on the ground and takes over the work into his own hands: but in case this drops thro, I believe Sunday night will be our last service, and the Tent will be taken down Monday and shipped to Seattle. The Tent was made in Seattle, so in case Bro. Thompson sells the one here, he will wire ahead and have a new one ready by the time we get there. Bro. Thompson is expecting to travel there by car--it will take at least a week--whether we shall accompany him or go by train am not yet sure.

Your good letter of the 12th to hand with thanks. Regarding questions: I have not had any further talk with Bro. Thompson recently including "Sov" in the sets to be sold in Seattle: am not sure how strongly he feels on the matter--he is so erratic and changeable, one never can tell just where he is: he has had little or no education, but is quick to pick up things and has acquired a good vocabulary and delivery by observing other speakers: but he is severely handicapped by lacking a trained mind which can think in logical order: the moment I lay down a premise and say "therefore" to draw a conclusion, he waves his hand and says "Speculation." When I quote a Scripture, he answers, "Yes, I know, but there is this on the other side", and quotes another--often one that has no relevancy at all to what we were discussing. He is clear as a bell on the total depravity of man: his utter Impotency, and is agreed with me on the will: says he believes in Sovereignty. & Eternal Election, but he bases this on God's foreknowledge of our faith: he rejects Reprobation in toto. Concerning my book as a whole (which he has never read--says he hasn't read thro a single book in his library) he says there must be something wrong with it as it divides God's people.

With regards to my writing other works, I hope to, I want to, but what is God's will in the matter I know not: it may be that He desires a wider circulation of those I have already written, and will keep me moving around from place to place to this end: by His grace I am keeping up my "Gen" [Genesis] articles, and these are nearing completion, so by the end of this year, DV, there should be another book ready for the market.

Please fill the following orders:

Mr. M.L. Hackett, 490 27th Street, Oakland, Cal.
4 copies of "7 Sayings".
Mrs. C.M. Holloway, 1832 Francisco St., Berkeley, Cal.
1 copy of "7 Sayings" & 1 copy of "Sov."
Mrs. Kolling, 3054 Georgia St., Oakland, Cal.
1 copy of "Sov."
Mrs. J.E. Rakistraw, 2518 Dana St., Berkeley, Cal.
1 copy of "7 Sayings".
Mr. Thos. Jones, Box 114, Fort Laramie, Wyoming
1 copy of "Sov." & 1 copy of "Inspr" in cloth

To each below here send one complete set, including "Sov.":

Mrs. C.A. Roberts, 307-11 Pacific Building, Oakland, Cal.
Mrs. Wm. Schleter, 2206 Grove St., Berkeley, Cal.
Mrs. Coomes, 1307 Castro St., Oakland, Cal.
Miss Nelson, 1618 Castro St., Oakland, Cal.

If you can, send "Sov" with the other books, but if "Sov" is not yet to hand, send the sets without it, and the "Sov" later: Mrs. Holloway's and Mrs. Jones' orders you can holdover until "Sov" can be supplied.

Mrs. Pink encloses her check for $41.35 ($15.10 for April 4 invoice; $26.25 for the above orders: the complete sets including Sov. being figured at $4.50 net--which according to invoices rec'd pays up everything to date--please say in your next if this is correct), which, together with her last check and mine for $15.00 makes over $100 this month: trust this will help you out: we shall pray regarding B.T.D. [Bible Truth Depot] finances: of late finances here have fallen off considerably and it will cost us a good deal to move to Seattle.

With best wishes,
Yrs by Grace,
AWP

INDEX

(References are according to month, day and year of letter)

Books and Pamphlets--Pink's

Pink says he is running low on book, so he is offering sets without it. 10/4/20; 10/9/20
Pink says H.A. Ironside is against the book. 1/17/21
Pink says Alesor Marshall is against the book 1/17/21
Pink says he is running short on the first edition--almost out. 2/3/21
Pink says he does not favor printing 1000 in second edition because little demand later on. Books are bound to drop with other things. 2/8/21
Pink says he is happy over the prices for binding the second edition. He also says he has gone over the whole manuscript for new material for the book. He is grateful for it. 3/2/21
Pink gives further word on binding. 3/18/21
Pink hopes new edition will be ready by end of April. 3/25/21
Pink hopes new edition will be out soon, but doesn't see much demand for it in Oakland. 3/28/21
Pink says Brother Thompson does not want Pink to sell the book in Seattle. 4/7/21
Pink says he is hoping to hear the book is in the hands of the binders now. 4/11/21
Pink reports no recent discussions with Brother Thompson about including the book in sets to sell in Seattle. 4/21/21

Threefold Salvation 7/28/20

The Way of Salvation 2/28/21; 3/7/21; 3/18/21

The Wrath of God 3/7/21

Your Correct Weight 3/7/21

Books, Periodicals and Pamphlets Other Than Pink's

The Berean Expositor (periodical)
Pink wants 1920 issues in cloth. 1/18/21; 1/30/21

HBT (no name given for this)
Pink asks Herendeen to renew this for him. 1/21/21

Help and Food
Pink says this magazine now publishing a report of open Bible readings in the Gospel. Also publishing a report of a meeting in Oakland last September on Romans 9 and 10 in which Brother C. Crain was the main speaker and in which A.W. Pink had a small part asking Brother Crain some pointed questions. 3/18/21
Pink answers Herendeen's question concerning which issues contain Romans 9 and 10 material. 4/7/21

Leviticus by C.H. Mackintosh 1/30/21

News and Truths
Pink asks Herendeen to send his copies. 1/21/21

Our Hope
A.C. Gabelein's periodical which has been running Pink's articles on Genesis.
Pink asks Herendeen to send his copies. 1/21/21
H.A. Ironside urges A.C. Gabelein to stop publishing Pink's articles on Genesis in this periodical. 2/28/21; 3/2/21
Pink reports he has taken fifty new subscriptions for this periodical while at Oakland. 4/7/21
Pink acknowledges a letter from A.C. Gabelein thanking him for the subscriptions to this magazine. 4/14/21

Things To Come by Bullinger? 1/30/21

Wonderful Word
Pink asks Herendeen to send his copies. 1/21/21

Denominations; Groups of Believers, etc.

Brethren 8/30/20: 9/15/20; 1/17/21 1/21/21; 1/30/21; 2/8/21; 3/2/21

Open Bible 1/17/21; 1/30/21; 2/14/21

Church of the Open Door 8/10/20

Presbyterian 2/14/21

Miscellaneous Items

Pink ordered a Hebrew grammar book. 7/28/20
Pink's house. 7/28/20; 8/5/20
Pink's personality. 9/22/20
Theosophy. 1/30/21
God provides an apartment. 2/23/21
Pink's comments on the work of chiropractor. 3/7/21; 3/12/21
Clergy permit--Pink still trying to get one. 3/12/21;

Persons--Well-Known

John Brown
a well-known evangelist who held meetings in Oakland while Pink was there. 11/17/21; 1/18/21; 1/30/21; 2/14/21

Bullinger
9/15/20
1/30/21
10/4/20 Pink says Dr. Pratt is a Bullingerite.
1/21/21 Alesor Marshall accuses Pink of "Bullingerism on" the subject of Limited Atonement.

J.N. Darby (JND)
Pink asks Herendeen to send book by JND. 3/25/21

A.C. Gabelein (ACG)

Pink says he is to be at Riverside, CA, at end of week. 7/28/20

Pink reports he saw him in Los Angeles and he was very cordial to Pink, asking him to save August 29th to preach in Church of the Open Door. 8/10/20

Pink mentions letter from ACG and says he is friendly disposed toward Pink. 2/8/21

Mrs. Pink says H.A. Ironside has written ACG accusing Pink of "damnable heresy," saying Pink is stating that hell is paved with babies. Ironside has told ACG that he is wrong to publish Pink's Genesis articles in "Our Hope" and that he must stop. Pink has brought in innumerable subscriptions to the magazine. 2/28/21

Pink thanks Herendeen for returning ACG letters. 3/2/21

Pink says that one of the women from the auditorium where H.A. Ironside was preaching in Oakland had told Mrs. Thompson that ACG had replied to Ironside's letter against Pink. He stated that if it was true that Pink was preaching false doctrine, he would cease publishing Pink's articles, would break fellowship with him, and would refuse to speak on the same platform with him. He said he was going to write Pink about the matter. Pink reports there is no letter from ACG yet. 3/2/21

Pink says he has not heard from ACG yet. 3/7/21

Pink reports no word from ACG yet, but a man from H.A. Ironside's assembly is going around showing people a letter he claims to have received from ACG in an effort to prejudice people against Pink. 3/12/21

Pink says he has no word from ACG yet--no news is good news. 4/7/21

Pink says he has sent fifty subscriptions to ACG's magazine since in Oakland, which should sweeten ACG. 4/7/21

Pink just received a letter from ACG in which he thanked Pink for the subscriptions and had nothing unpleasant to say. 4/14/21

H.A. Ironside (HAI)

Pink expects him back in Oakland by the end of the week. 8/23/20

Pink expects Ironside back in Oakland next week, and then they will discuss the book on sovereignty or the subject of sovereignty. 8/27/20

Pink says Ironside will be in Oakland for the annual Brethren conference at the end of the week, and he expects to have it out with him on sovereignty and reprobation. 8/30/20

Pink says little opportunity yet to talk to Ironside. 9/7/20

Pink marvels that Brother Thompson asked him to speak at the tent and not Ironside. 9/15/20

Pink reports tension between Ironside and Brother Thompson and Pink. 1/17/21; 1/18/21

Pink says Ironside is cool to him when they meet. 1/30/21

Pink tells of instance of being questioned during a service in the tent by a friend of Ironside. 2/8/21

Pink says Ironside is warning others against the tent. 2/8/21

Pink says the people of Ironside's association are afraid to come to the tent. 2/14/21

Pink says Ironside is now speaking three times a week at the Gospel Auditorium instead of his previous once a week. He is speaking on Zechariah and finding it hard to hold his crowd. 2/23/21

Mrs. Pink says Ironside has written Gabelein saying Pink was teaching"damnable heresy," and that Pink had said "the way to hell is paved with babies." Ironside also told ACG that he was doing a great wrong in publishing Pink's articles on Genesis in "Our Hope." He advises him to stop printing Pink. 2/28/21

Pink says that Ironside gave an address last Friday evening on Zechariah, and that two of the brethren from his group stood outside Pink's tent and sought to talk people into going to the Ironside meetings. 3/2/21

Pink restates what Mrs. Pink said in 2/28/21 letter. 3/2/21

Pink says a man named Matlock from Ironside's group is showing people a letter supposedly from Gabelein to prejudice them against Pink. 3/12/21

Pink says that Ironside carefully altered the statements of his friend C. Crain on Romans 9-10 discussion at Gospel Auditorium in Oakland in Fall of 1920. 4/7/21

<u>Philip Mauro</u>

Pink mentions his teaching on healing. 7/29/20

Pink mentions his teaching on the kingdom as being held by teachers at the Institute (which institute not clear). 8/10/20

Pink assumes a letter from Herendeen from a Mr. M is from Mauro. 3/2/21

<u>C.H. Mackintosh</u> (CHM) well known Brethren writer of Britain 1/30/21

<u>R. A. Torrey</u>

8/10/20

Persons--Not Well-Known

<u>Barbour, Mr. and Mrs</u>. of Asheville, NC 3/2/21

<u>Brown, Dr.</u> of Spartanburg, SC 10/4/20; 3/25/21

<u>Burd, C. and A</u>. of PA 3/12/21

<u>Catherwood, Dr.</u> of Santa Barbara, CA 10/4/20

Clarence, Brother of PA 9/22/20

Cole, Brother of Mortons Gap, KY 3/2/21

Cowles 2/3/21; 3/2/21; 3/12/21

Crain, C 8/10/20; 8/23/20; 8/27/20; 8/30/20; 9/7/20; 10/8/20; 10/16/20; 1/18/21; 1/30/21; 4/7/21; 3/18/21;

Crane, Mr. 8/30/20

Daniels, Brother 2/8/21

Dean, Brother 1/30/21

Evans, D. of Chicago, IL 4/21/21

Farr, Rev. of CA 8/10/20

Francis, Dr., Garden Grove, CA 7/28/20

Grant, Brother 8/30/20

Haddon, Rev. of CA 8/10/20

Herendeen, Norman of PA 7/29/20

Horton, Mr. of Church of the Open Door, CA 8/10/20

Hunt, Brother of Vancouver 9/15/20

Jurkin, Mr. of Garden Grove, CA 8/5/20

Kilgore, Brother 8/13/20

Lee, Brother of Bible Institute of Los Angeles 7/28/20

Lee, Harry of Garden Grove, CA 7/29/20

Lewis, Gwynne, Riverside CA 9/22/20

Pink says Thompson came and talked to him about the Brethren. 8/30/20

Pink says Thompson agrees with him on sovereignty, God's love only for the elect, and that he is half convinced on reprobation. 8/30/20

Pink says Thompson goes all the way with him on sovereignty, eternal reprobation, and limited atonement. 9/7/20

See also 9/15/20.

Thompson invited Pink back to Oakland. 9/22/20

Thompson not a man of means. 10/4/20; 4/7/21

Thompson has tension with Ironside. 1/17/21

Thompson with Pink in clash with Alesor Marshall. 1/21/20

Thompson has given away all literature from Herendeen. 1/30/21

Thompson has received another urgent call to come to Seattle for meetings. 2/3/21

Thompson plans to leave Oakland February 15 for six weeks (evidently for meetings in Seattle) with Pink in charge at tent, and he will return the first week of April when Pink would then go to Seattle for a couple of months (evidently to speak to those Thompson has reached in Seattle). 2/3/21

Pink describes Thompson's handling of an evening service in the tent. 2/8/21

Pink says the majority of the church folks were mad because Thompson continued meetings in the tent while John Brown was in Oakland. He had been asked to close while Brown was there, but had refused. 2/14/21

Thompson to leave for Seattle this week for three weeks. 2/14/21

Thompson now in Seattle and Pink has not heard from him. 2/23/21

Thompson still in Seattle and doesn't know when he shall return. 2/28/21

Thompson expects to be back from Seattle this week. 3/7/21

Thompson has returned from Seattle and intends to see letter supposedly from A.C. Gabelein which is being passed around by a man named Matlock from H.A. Ironside's assembly. 3/12/21

Thompson lunched with Pink and Pink prodded him for not paying Herendeen what he owed. 3/18/21

Pink calls Thompson a "queer fish" because he wavers from day to day on sovereignty--one day he is for it, and the next day he says Pink is "riding a hobby horse." Pink says he also wavers on leaving Oakland. 3/18/21

Pink still prodding Thompson to pay Herendeen, and he finally did. 3/28/21

Pink spoke to Thompson about balance still owed Herendeen. 4/7/21

Thompson got a wire from a Brother Whitney in Seattle. Thompson wired Whitney to level lot, etc. 4/7/21

Thompson erratic with people about going to Seattle or staying in Oakland. 4/11/21

Thompson reluctant to close work in Oakland; he may sell his tent to Brother Pietsch, a former member of Ironside's assembly. 4/21/21

Pink says Thompson is doctrinally very erratic--not a trained thinker--illogical--clear on total depravity, but bases election on foreknowledge of faith. He rejects reprobation. He never has read Pink's book on sovereignty or read through a single book in his library. He says Pink's book on sovereignty must be wrong because it divides God's people. 4/21/21

<u>Troy, Brother</u> of Brooklyn, NY 9/15/20

<u>Tucker, Brother</u>, Pasadena, CA 9/15/20

<u>Whitney, Guy</u>, of Seattle, WA 9/15/20; 10/4/20; 10/16/20; 4/7/21; 4/11/21; 4/21/21

Winstead, L.M., a pastor of Madisonville, KY 1/2/21; 2/3/21

Scripture References

Psalm 34 8/23-20

Zechariah 2/23/21

Matthew 5:10 8/10/20

John 3:16 1/21/21; 1/30/21; 3/2/21

John 17:9 1/21/21

Acts 9:26 8/30/20

Romans 9 3/21/21

Romans 9-10 3/18/21

I Timothy 2:1-6 1/21/21

Revelation 3:21 1/30/21

Sermons

1. Pink preached on "Three-fold Salvation" on July 27, 1920. 7/28/20

2. Pink preached on "A Sinner's Ruin" to a union service at Orange, CA. 7/10/20

3. Pink preached on "Grace" at an afternoon service at a Congregational Church. 8/23/20

4. Pink preached on "The Way of Salvation" at the first meeting in the tent in Oakland. 8/23/20

5. Pink says he intends to expound doctrine in the tent at Oakland. 8/23/20

6. Pink preached on "Justification" on Wednesday night at Riverside, CA. 10/4/20

7. Pink preached on "Grace" at Sunday morning service at Pasadena in Pratt's church on Sunday, October 3, 1920, and then preached on "The Cross" on Sunday evening. 10/4/20

8. Pink preached on"Sanctification" on October 7, 1920. 10/8/20

9. Pink expects to begin second time in the tent on February 1, 1921 and will preach on the Gospel of John. 1/17/21

10. Pink's text on January 17, 1921 was Hebrews 11. 1/18/21

11. Pink says he gave seven addresses last week on Matthew 7, dealing mainly with the dispensational scope. 1/30/21

12. Pink says he preached on Mark 16:16, dwelling on "...he that believeth not shall be damned." 1/30/21

13. Pink says he preached on Matthew 8 at a dispensational meeting. 1/30/21

14. Pink says he did start a series on the gospel of John in the tent on Wednesday, February 2, 1921. 2/3/21

15. Pink preached on Luke's gospel, Christ the Son of man, emphasizing the uniqueness of Christ's humanity. 2/3/21

16. Pink reiterates he is still expounding John 1, mentioning 1:13. 2/8/21

17. Pink says he spoke on Zacchaeus Sunday evening and many were deeply stirred. 2/23/21

18. Pink says he has spent fifty hours speaking on John's gospel and is only in John 4. 3/2/21

19. Pink says he departs from John on Sunday nights and has spoken almost entirely on "Man's Ruin," using such subjects and texts as Mark 16:16, the Prodigal Son, Blind Bartimaeuss, Zacchaeus, and Judgment Day (Acts 17:30-31). 3/7/21

20. Pink says he will complete John 6 tonight. 3/18/21

21. Pink says he spoke at the afternoon and evening services yesterday on "The Resurrection of the Christian." 3/28/21

22. Pink says he spoke yesterday afternoon on John 13 (footwashing) and on "The Lord's Return" from John 14 in the evening. 4/11/21

23. Pink says he is not cut out for "short and breezy talks" in the place of sermons. 4/11/21

24. Pink says he has preached 77 sermons this trip. 4/11/21

Theology

Annihilation 8/10/20; 8/13/20

Depravity of man 4/21/21

Election 4/21/21

Eternal Punishment 8/13/20

Final Reconciliation 8/10/20

Foreordination of all things 1/21/21

Humanity of Christ 2/3/21

Limited Atonement 9/27/20; 1/21/21

Open Meeting 8/30/20

Prophecy 8/30/20

Reprobation 8/30/20; 9/27/20; 1/17/21; 4/21/21

Sovereignty 8/27/20; 8/30/20; 9/27/20; 1/18/21; 3/18/21

Tongues 8/30/20

Universal Reconciliation 7/28/20

Will 3/25/21

World 1/30/21; 3/2/21

Writing--Pink's Thoughts about His

1. Pink says writing not going to be easy as a travelling preacher--too many demands by the people. 7/28/20

2. Pink says he is thronged and writing is difficult. 7/29/20

3. Pink says he is convinced the Lord would have him devote at least one-third of his time studying and writing. 9/22/20

4. Pink says again he is convinced the Lord would have him devote at least one-third of his time studying and writing, but believes this will be more difficult as time goes on. 10/8/20

5. Pink says he expects many open doors in the future, along with a doubling and tripling of the sale of his books, but does hope and expect to continue studying and writing. He says he has read seven books in the last two weeks. 10/8/20

6. Pink says studying is hard (finding time). He has just finished an article on Genesis for "Our Hope." 2/8/21

7. Pink says he has not studied Romans any further since leaving Swengel, PA. 3/18/21

8. Pink says the sale and writing of books is more important than his oral ministry. 4/7/21

9. Regarding the writing of other books, Pink says, "I hope to, I want to, but what is God's will in the matter I know not." Pink thinks maybe God wants a wider circulation of what he has already written as he keeps moving around from place to place. He states he is keeping up his Genesis articles, and they are nearing completion and thus a new book will be available for market. 4/21/21

BOOKS BY DR. RICHARD P. BELCHER

Richbarry Press, Box 302, Columbia, SC 29202

(a price list is available on request)

THEOLOGY

A Comparison of Dispensationalism and Covenant Theology 46 pages, ISBN # 0-925703-52-4 An objective analysis and comparison of two major systems of theology.

A Layman's Guide to the Lordship Controversy 123 pages, ISBN # 0-925703-13-3 In this work the author aids the layman in coming to an understanding of the controversy by summarizing the two positions on this important issue--the Lordship and the non-Lordship views. He then provides an excellent critique of the non-lordship position based on Scripture.

A Layman's Guide to the Sabbath Question 161 pages, ISBN # 0-925703-43-5 Co-authored by Richard P. Belcher, Jr., this book presents and compares three current views of the Sabbath -- The Seventh Day view, the Christian Sabbath view, and the Lord's Day view.

A Layman's Guide to the Inerrancy Debate 80 pages, ISBN # 0-925703-50-8 A series of essays answering key questions and objections concerning the doctrine of Biblical inerrancy.

I Believe in Inerrancy 54 pages, ISBN # 0-925703-24-9 A Biblical, historical and theological presentation of the doctrine of the inspiration of Scripture especially prepared for the layman but helpful to all.

GREEK HELPS

A Practical Approach to the Greek New Testament 52 pages (8 1/2 X 11 in size) ISBN # 0-925703-53-2 An introduction to a practical use of the Greek NT helpful and useful for both those who have or have not had Greek.

Diagramming the Greek New Testament 62 pages, (8 1/2 X 11 in size) ISBN # 0-925703-54-0 A self-teaching manual to help one learn to diagram the Greek NT.

Doing an Effective Greek Word Study 23 pages ISBN # 0-925703-57-5 A manual which seeks to chart the procedure for doing a Greek word study from the Classical, Hellenistic, Patriarchal, etc, sources.

Doing Textual Criticism in the Greek New Testament 25 pages, ISBN # 0-925703-56-7 A manual which seeks to explain in a simple and understandable way the principles and practice of textual criticism in the Greek NT.

Doing Biblical Exegesis 10 pages, ISBN # 0-925703-55-9 A manual which traces the basic steps in doing Biblical exegesis in a minor or major manner.

MINISTRY HELPS

Teaching Helps in Psalms 53 pages (8 1/2 X 11 size) ISBN # 0-925703-19-2 A doctrinal study guide of Psalms with a clear preachable or teachable outline which can easily be divided into individual outlines. Doctrinal areas covered include the Scriptures, God, man, worship, etc. Background material is presented also in an introductory sermon outline.

Ministry Helps in Isaiah 132 pages (8 1/2 X 11 size) A study guide of Isaiah with a clear preachable or teachable outline which can easily be divided into individual outlines following the subjects of the sin of God's people, the judgment of God's people, the solution to the problem of God's people, the future blessings of God's people, etc. Background material is presented also in an introductory sermon outline.

Ministry Helps in Hosea (8 1/2 X 11 size) A study guide of Hosea with a clear preachable or teachable outline which can easily be divided into individual outlines following the theme of Old Covenant Failure--New Covenant Hope. Background material is presented also in an introductory sermon outline.

Teaching Helps in Malachi 38 pages (8 1/2 X 11 size) ISBN # 0-925703-63-X A study guide of Malachi with a clear preachable or teachable outline which can easily be divided into individual outlines following the theme of the burden of Malachi. Background material is presented also in an introductory sermon outline.

Ministry Helps in John 60 pages (8 1/2 X 11 size) ISBN # 0-925703-18-4 A study guide of John with a clear preachable or teachable outline which can easily be divided into individual outlines following the theme of the Word Christ Jesus as presented, pondered, persecuted etc. Background material is presented also in an introductory sermon outline.

Ministry Helps in Acts 72 pages (81/2 X 11 size) ISBN # 0-925703-62-1 A study guide of Acts with a clear preachable or teachable outline which can easily be divided into individual outlines following the theme of six provisions God made for world evangelization. Background material is presented also in an introductory sermon outline.

Teaching Helps in I Corinthians (8 1/2 X 11 size) A study guide of I Corinthians with a clear preachable or teachable outline which can easily be divided into individual outlines following the theme of unity and sound doctrine. Background material is also provided in a preachable introductory sermon outline.

Teaching Helps in II Corinthians 38 pages (8 1/2 X 11 Size) ISBN # 0-925703-15-X A study guide of II Corinthians with a clear preachable or teachable outline which can easily be divided into individual outlines following the theme of New Testament Ministry. Background material is presented also in an introductory sermon outline.

Teaching Helps in Hebrews 56 pages (81/2 X 11 size) ISBN # 925703-16-8 A study guide of Hebrews with a clear preachable or teachable outline which can easily be divided into individual outlines following the theme of the superiority of the New Covenant. Background material is presented also in an introductory sermon outline.

Teaching Helps in James 64 pages (81/2 X 11 size) ISBN # 0-925703-17-6 A study guide of James with a clear preachable or teachable outline which can easily be divided into individual outlines following the theme of practical Christian living. Background material is presented also in an introductory sermon outline.

Teaching Helps in I Peter 76 pages (8 1/2 X 11 size) A study guide of I Peter with a clear preachable or teachable outline which can easily be divided into individual outlines following the them of the glorious salvation possessed by God's covenant people.

PREACHING HELPS

Preaching the Gospel - A Theological Perspective 58 pages ISBN # 0-925703-21-4 Using I Corinthians 1-4 and II Timothy 3:1-4:4 as the basis of study, the author sets forth the nature of the gospel we must preach and the nature of the methods we must employ. He argues we are not free to determine the nature or content of the gospel nor the method of presentation. Failure to understand this is what has led to the modern demise of Biblical preaching.

Preaching the Gospel - A Personal Method 61 pages ISBN # 0-925703-20-6 This is a book that will not only help the beginning preacher who wishes to build proper preaching habits, but it will give aid also to the experienced preacher to sharpen and improve his skills.

THEOLOGICAL NOVELS

A Journey in Grace 154 pages ISBN # 0-925703-11-7
This is a theological novel--the story of a young pastor with a typical twentieth century theology and his pursuit of a burning theological question which was triggered in his first experience with a pulpit search committee. He cannot and does not rest until he has answered the challenge of the question, "Young man, are you a Calvinist?"

A Journey in Purity 215 pages ISBN # 0-925703-39-7
This is the sequel to the novel "A Journey in Grace." It is the story of the same pastor in his difficult and heart-breaking struggle to bring purity to the corrupt church he pastors. This book identifies with any pastor or church member alike who has ever wrestled with the principles of church discipline.

HISTORICAL STUDIES

Seventeenth Century Baptist Confessions of Faith 56 pages ISBN # 0-925703-23-0 Co-authored by Anthony Mattia. A discussion and refutation of the claim that the First London Confession in its 1644 and 1646 editions has a different view of the Law the Second London Confession of 1689.

BOOKS ABOUT ARTHUR W. PINK

A.W. Pink - Predestination 136 pages ISBN # 0-925703-51-6 An analysis of the central theological theme of A.W. Pink. This work uses the Pink sources to set forth his views of predestination, election and reprobation.

A.W. Pink - Born to Write 165 pages This is the second edition of a biography of the life of Pink which appeared in 1982 with a limited number of copies available. The author not only presents the facts of Pink's life, with several chapters of new material possessed by no other biographer, but he also analyzes the life of Pink--his unique personality, his rejection by men, his study methodology, his withdrawal, and his life of isolation during his final years.

Arthur W. Pink - Letters from Spartanburg 1917-1920 287 pages ISBN # 1-88-3265-00-2 A series of about a hundred letters written by Pink when he was pastor of Northside Baptist Church in Spartanburg, SC during the years of 1917-1920. This was the period he wrote his best known book "The Sovereignty of God." Edited by Dr. Belcher with a complete index for easy use in tracing items of special interest.

Arthur W. Pink - Letters of an Itinerant Preacher 1920-21 93 pages A series of letters written by Pink when he was an itinerant preacher working mostly in California. This was a period when he was wrestling with God's will for his life, either to continue a public ministry or devote himself exclusively to a writing ministry. Edited by Dr. Belcher with a complete index for easy use in tracing items of special interest.

REPRINTS OF OLDER BOOKS

Luther Rice - Pioneer in Missions and Education 125 pages ISBN # 1-883265-07-X This is an old biography of Luther Rice by Edward B. Pollard and Daniel Gurden Stevens, first published in the first part of this twentieth century. It details the life of Rice and the strong but sometimes unknown contribution he made to the cause of modern missions and education in the life of Baptists of America. Prepared for publication by Richard P. Belcher.